MOODSET

HOW TO CREATE A PERFORMANCE CLIMATE THAT INSPIRES EXCELLENCE

TIM WIGHAM

authorHOUSE®

AuthorHouse™ UK
1663 Liberty Drive
Bloomington, IN 47403 USA
www.authorhouse.co.uk
Phone: UK TFN: 0800 0148641 (Toll Free inside the UK)
       UK Local: (02) 0369 56322 (+44 20 3695 6322 from outside the UK)

Published by AuthorHouse 08/01/2022

ISBN: 978-1-7283-7400-0 (sc)
ISBN: 978-1-7283-7399-7 (e)

Foreword

The 'servant leader' concept is one that trips easily off the tongue and is blithely used by many in positions of authority who actually have very little idea of what is genuinely involved. It just sounds good, a neat encapsulation of perceived humility and an inclusive approach. But if there is one man who epitomises the term, it is Tim Wigham.

This is not to say that Tim does not and cannot lead with authority and purpose when required - he is a former Royal Marines Officer after all, and a formidable physical presence having remained disgustingly fit and remarkably mentally disciplined in the years since he left the Armed Forces. True leadership is, after all, a nuanced affair, much of it based around knowing when to step up and intervene, and I have personally witnessed Tim take charge in dynamic situations to extraordinary effect. But as a rule, his approach can be encapsulated in a single sentence. "I am here to make you more effective as a group, as individuals, as leaders - let's work together to make that happen." He essentially places himself at the disposal of the myriad organisations that call upon his services as a mentor and coach, and the end results speak volumes. His diligence, vast knowledge, and experience are all combined to great effect, but at the heart of it all is a genuine desire to serve those he leads.

This approach is not just some ethereal desire to help others, it is based on real structure. And that is what is so neatly encapsulated in this book. His summary of how to create an efficient culture is, quite frankly, brilliant. Having worked for twenty years or so in the same field as Tim - essentially trying to define and implement what makes an efficient team or organisation - his distillation of what is required is the best I've ever seen. It is a brilliant assessment of what you need to do to become highly effective (I won't spoil it for you by stating it here, but suffice to say that when he devised it I thought "Yes!", and then immediately felt annoyed that I hadn't come up with it myself).

His approach to leadership and team culture have been applied in a vast range of environments, from elite sports teams to multi-national corporations, from school groups to hard-bitten military operatives. The consistent feedback from all of these individuals and teams is how transformative the coaching has been, and (without wishing to embarrass him) what a thoroughly decent human being he is. The latter is not to be underestimated, after all leadership starts with the individual and his/her personal standards. I can vouch with the confidence of knowing him for nearly three decades, that Tim's character is genuinely beyond reproach, and his enthusiasm for what he does is marvellous to behold.

It's all in here, so get stuck in and enjoy this book. The following chapters are a neat summation of decades of study, of what works and what does not, of genuine, hands on, practical leadership training and - significantly - applying that theory to real life situations. It is a brilliant description of how to get the job done, how to forge a culture that is truly effective, and create a team that operates to the very highest standards.

I'll finish with a very brief story that - for me - encapsulates Tim, and indeed his approach to helping us all achieve our goals. A couple of years ago I was attempting a truly daunting endurance challenge, and needed someone to coach me, to act as a mentor in the darkest hours before the dawn, and to shape my attitude and approach. There was only one man who I thought to call, and his approach throughout typified an attitude and an expertise that has achieved so much for so many. He had one aim, one goal, and that was to leave no stone unturned in getting me to the finish line. Tellingly, as we staggered the last few steps of the marathon, he quietly peeled away into the darkness so I could cross the line alone and receive the acclaim. A moment that, for me anyway, embodies Tim as an individual, and indeed is the perfect example of what a servant leader is all about.

It's such a privilege to be asked to write this foreword, and now I wish you well as you too begin the journey of the book itself. It is a truly brilliant piece of work.

Monty Halls
- Broadcaster, Leader, Author, Adventurer, Entrepreneur, Marine.

Contents

This book is for my children
LEOLA, ZACHARY, CAYLA

Thanks for teaching me the meaning
of love, and for helping me understand
the importance of mood!

"Mood is our inner music, moodset is the playlist that we create and choose!"

Introduction

I have been immensely privileged in my life to serve and lead teams at school level, in the military, and in business. As a performance coach I have been inspired by many teams in many sectors. I have learned many lessons so I want to share what I can.

I am a husband, and father of three children. A role that truly raises the stakes of servant leadership.

Attending boarding school at a young age, I was immediately interested in social dynamics and team interaction even though I did not consciously deliberate on it at the time. What interested me most was the idea of camaraderie, respect, fairness, and collective will.

I noticed and experienced poor leadership which often enabled or even endorsed various forms of bullying. This triggered an internal determination to make a positive difference to any culture I had an opportunity to join. It ignited a fire inside me to learn and lead an approach that accepts the possibility of failure in the pursuit of growth, allows authentic expression in a safe environment, and encourages vulnerability to be real about the challenges we all face.

When I was given the responsibility to be Head of House at secondary school. I intuitively sensed the delicate balancing act required to maintain order and morale, to inspire performance but also to ensure protection, to allow traditional seniority but also to nurture future leaders.

A leader in the same role many years before me had maintained a daily journal to capture leadership observations. I resumed the practice as it was clear to me that each year-group would face similar challenges and we could build on previous growth to improve community and camaraderie in our boarding house.

Creating an atmosphere which inspires individual flair and collective flow became my mission, and that focus has remained with me to this day.

Creating an atmosphere which inspires individual flair and collective flow became my mission, and that focus has remained with me to this day.

There were a couple of incidents at school where I made decisions with the intent to reduce interference from disruptive elements to maintain the conditions for overall optimal flow. I learned valuable lessons from the ripple-effect of those decisions. I also realised how delicate any collaboration climate can be.

Much like climate control in a car, climate control in a group requires constant attention.

Much like climate control in a car, climate control in a group requires constant attention.

Sport has always played a significant part in my life. Running, rugby, and latterly crossfit are the sports I am most passionate about. Sport was given equal importance to academics at my secondary school, Falcon College. It was a critical crucible for the formation of character, collaboration, and courage. I was part of my age-group rugby squad all the way through school and was a team captain in my final year.

I learned massive lessons about moodset during that time. It was my job to ensure the team ran onto each field with clear eyes and a full heart. If necessary, I had to help the team find another gear when the chips were down. My behaviour, and my body language, was reflected by the team. In return, when I made mistakes, my teammates were there to clean up the mess.

Something that still gives me goose bumps is the school war cry. Not just my old school but all schools in Southern Africa, especially before and after a match. There was one school called Plumtree in Zimbabwe; their war cry was the chorus from the warrior song *Impi* by Johnny Clegg. When we played against Plumtree, the hair went up on the back of our necks and our senses were heightened to fever pitch. Inspiration was off the charts and moodset was in overdrive. Anyone who wants to trace the source of the rugby pool of excellence in places like South Africa and New Zealand, need only watch a school match on YouTube to experience climate, commitment, and culture at the next level.

Anyone who wants to trace the source of rugby excellence in places like South Africa and New Zealand, need only watch a school match on YouTube to experience commitment and culture at the next level.

After school I applied to become an officer in the Royal Marines. I was fortunate to get through the selection process and to complete young-officer (YO) training. I served for eight years and gained many reference points for excellence in adversity. Perhaps more-so than any other environment, the marines explicitly train a commando mindset and a commando method, this method includes discipline and teamwork. Commando moodset however, is learned through 'felt' experience.

The feeling of 'belonging', forged through the commando crucible, became a valuable reference point as I progressed through professional life.

As a commando leader on operations, I was privileged to learn from non-commissioned officers (NCOs) who had seen a lot more action than I ever would, about how to maintain morale - a key principle of war. Cheerfulness and unselfishness are expectations of any marine. This means that no matter the discomfort, team members stay positive. I saw this in Northern Ireland and Sierra Leone in the 1990s. When the risks were real, the fun remained frequent. This sets the mood to 'hopeful and happy' no matter the surrounding difficulty.

Cheerfulness and unselfishness are
expectations of any marine.

My military time has allowed me to put anything and everything that goes 'wrong' into perspective. A fellow Bootneck once said to me; "Take your job seriously but not yourself!"

"Take your job seriously but not yourself!"

When faced with the trivialities that account for ninety-nine percent of our daily anxiety, I remind myself to stay positive and ask; "Is someone likely to die?" If the answer is "no", I try to take a deep breath and 'crack on'. Another marine euphemism for 'keep going'.

Moodset is very closely linked to our surroundings, our environment, and our felt experience. To this end, I enrolled in a full-time MBA as a transitionary year at the end of my eight years in the Royal Marines. One of the reasons I targeted this experience was that I knew it would be uncomfortable, but I also knew I would be surrounded by motivated young professionals striving for accelerated progress. My mood would be energised by my peers.

My mood would be energised by my peers.

That is how it played out and my MBA year was transformational on many levels. Most interesting in hindsight, is the fact that I had two very different experiences with the two different syndicate groups I joined at different stages of the year. Building on that, I returned as a facilitator exactly ten years later, to introduce and run an annual breakaway for MBA students such that the ice-breaking and forming/storming process (Tuckman, 1965) could be accelerated, and a moodset for excellence could be established within the syndicates before commencing with the challenging assignments that come thick and fast after the induction week. This proved to be a gamechanger for faculty and students who often spent the entire first semester dealing with unnecessary friction and frustration due to ego and emotion.

My time at the Graduate School of Business helped me to transition from a military background into the commercial world, and I realised my passion lay in helping professional teams with their leadership, teamwork, and discipline. These were elements which I had been privileged to learn both at Falcon College and in the Royal Marines, so I set about building a brand to support professional teams.

> *I set about building a brand to*
> *support professional teams.*

My first experiment was *Gameplans*, or *Plan your Game*, which aspired to help sports teams unlock potential through mental toughness and mental skills. I was helping teams to work on their mindset for performance, and I was fortunate to be able to spend some time with many future Springbok stars who went on to win the Rugby World Cup in France 2007. I had seen interventions by the Royal Marines with England Rugby, so I adapted and transferred that good practice.

A key realisation (which should be common sense) for me, was that practical leadership tasks - whether navigating routes over a mountain, or solving riddles - build trust, camaraderie, and mutual respect way quicker than sitting in a classroom discussing theory.

> *Practical leadership tasks build trust,*
> *camaraderie, and mutual respect way*
> *quicker than sitting in a classroom.*

These challenges can strengthen mindset while also building a moodset of hope and inspiration based on reference points for team members who have witnessed resilience and collaboration in a variety of uncomfortable situations. What we feel tends to stay with us far longer than what we hear.

What we feel tends to stay with us
far longer than what we hear.

Working with provincial and national rugby squads in South Africa was an immense privilege and a time when I learned a huge amount about inspiring a mood for momentum. In fact, as a passionate life-long Springbok and Blitzbok supporter, I have seen and felt the hope, inspiration and celebration of a nation obsessed with its sporting heroes.

My TEDx Talk on Moodset references the 1995 RWC when Mandela wove his magic into the mix. In 2019, Siya Kolisi made history when he led the Springboks to victory in that unforgettable final. The documentary *Chasing the Sun* about the 2019 Boks is one of the most inspiring TV series I have ever watched. I recommend it to anyone who wants to believe in the power of hope, the power of sport, and the power of purpose.

As a side note, I was lucky enough to attend the 2007 RWC Final in Paris when the Springboks beat England. That set a positive mood and a strong period for the Boks.

Through my personal family network, I was introduced to an entrepreneur in 2003. He offered to acquire *Gameplans*, and we agreed a mutually fair growth plan while teambuilding with groups in corporate Southern Africa.

This was a challenging time for me personally and professionally. As such it was a period when I grew a huge amount as a facilitator of different groups. Three significant memories from that time positively affect my mood. One is meeting the woman who would become my wife, the second is that I learned about the power of movie making – a signature event we offered corporate groups, the third is that I decided to enrol in a series of coaching courses to qualify myself as a professional integral coach.

Through the investment I made in upskilling myself as a coach, I serendipitously met the founder of Exceed who happened to be in Cape Town. That meeting in 2006 began my journey with Exceed, now 16 years long. The lesson? Invest in your personal passion and professional purpose, and the universe conspires to help you succeed!

Invest in your personal passion and professional purpose, and the universe conspires to help you succeed!

My wife (then partner) and I decided to set up the Cape Leadership Centre in Cape Town in 2005. That included an outdoor leadership course where we ran breakaways for executive groups as well as fitness classes for enthusiasts in the Cape. I remember painting a large sign, 'Your Field of Dreams' to set the mood for all groups who came along.

Moodset is performance climate, which is driven by environmental cues such as what we see, hear, smell, taste, touch. In other words, moodset is what we sense when we arrive at any place, especially for the first time.

Environmental cues are critical for inspiration and hope. Moodset is mood sense! I still like to recce and set up any conference room where I will facilitate, well in advance. I strongly believe that the facilitator's mood sets the group mood, which in turn sets the tone for the session. Delegates sense preparation and organisation. They step into the moodset, the performance climate, the prevailing energy, which interweaves leadership and teamwork, fire and flow.

*Moodset is what we sense when we arrive
at any place, especially for the first time.
Performance climate interweaves leadership
and teamwork, fire and flow.*

Between 2007 and 2010 I experienced highs and lows akin to the Himalayas! I got married, which was a huge high, but then experienced the struggle of starting a family. That was a three-year low and setting a positive mood despite the constant setbacks was a massive challenge.

Faith, friends, and family played a big part in maintaining morale during that period. A key learning on reflection is the importance of resilience. We did not give up hope and we persevered with IVF until in 2010 we were blessed with our first child - a beautiful daughter.

I realise now that mindset, method and moodset were all crucial in the manifestation of this miracle. From doubt to determination, from dabbling to data and detail, and from depressed to delighted, the transformation of our family is a superb case study for a breakthrough of any kind.

On the work front, 2007 through 2012 was an incredibly steep learning curve. I committed to performance consulting within the energy sector and perhaps because of my parallel journeys as a student of coaching and a student of family, I was able to weave personal insight into professional inspiration.

For a diamond-dredging campaign offshore Namibia, I applied six-sigma principles and collaboration techniques to optimise the onshore performance climate for a client in Windhoek. The 'mood' room I established on the HR floor was a safe space for anyone to visit when looking to be inspired. It included quotes and artefacts to boost team members and allow them to distil ideas to help the team breakthrough barriers. We called it breakthrough performance (BTP) coaching and the breakaways that we facilitated were a big part of the breakthroughs.

*The 'mood' room I established on the
HR floor was a safe space for anyone to
visit when looking to be inspired.*

I have rarely if ever encountered a group that has not enjoyed or benefited from a breakaway from the normal work environment (be that home or a worksite). The simple ingredients of an offsite get-together with an agenda that includes indoor and outdoor interaction, along with a meal involving good food and wine, always serves to set a positive mood and a sense of belonging and benefit. If leaders influence the set up and are then influential by truly 'showing' up, a team breakaway can be a catalyst for accelerated transformation.

*A team breakaway can be a catalyst
for accelerated transformation.*

After my experience supporting the diamond industry, I was offered the opportunity to transfer to oil and gas. I seized the chance to ply my trade on offshore floaters and in hindsight I am glad that I sensed when a career-changing opportunity was being presented such that I could throw myself into it with 100% commitment.

My eighteen months on the GSF Explorer for Exceed supporting BP Angola, followed by eighteen months on the Eirik Raude supporting Tullow Ghana were formative experiences. I had zero previous experience in the O&G Industry which was a handicap as well as a massive advantage. The obvious handicap was a lack of technical knowledge, the benefit was objective perspective unencumbered by experience.

I was able to guide an agreed methodology around planning and learning without doubting the value of the activities. I also recorded everything because it was new to me. I asked the stupid questions, and I questioned what else could be done. Performance improvement methodology was enhanced, but performance moodset was also exposed as a critical factor on these campaigns. Leaders play a major role in moodset as we know, and I saw both extremes between those two campaigns.

> *Performance moodset was also exposed as*
> *a critical factor on these campaigns.*

Leaders are often unaware of their impact on the mood of those around them. Truth be told, when I reflected on my experiences of this recently for my 2021 TEDx Talk, I started to think about my own impact on my team and my family. I realised that we teach what we need to learn.

> *I realised that we teach what we need to learn.*

I am often a little withdrawn and aloof at home, so I want to raise the topic of moodset because I am as vulnerable as the next leader to lapses in awareness, and to spreading a bad mood to my own team if I'm not self-aware.

> *I am as vulnerable as the next leader to lapses*
> *in awareness, and to spreading a bad mood*
> *to my own team if I'm not self-aware.*

Unfortunately, mood is contagious and a bad mood spreads faster than a good one. I realised that even using 'moodset' as a trigger word, helped me to reboot after a busy day, and to put a smile on my face and a skip in my step to bring happiness to the atmosphere at home. It is a never-ending challenge but through repeated focus, like anything, it can be improved!

I realised that even using 'moodset' as a trigger word, helped me to reboot after a busy day, and to put a smile on my face and a skip in my step to bring happiness to the atmosphere at home.

By 2012, I was kick-starting performance-improvement campaigns for Exceed clients as a project manager. In this capacity, I conducted many culture and climate assessment visits and interviews. I count myself as very lucky to have completed these visits in Africa, Europe, the Middle East, and the Far East. Societal culture in these places is varied, plus each team has its own climate or moodset. This is affected by the diversity of its members, its location, the workscope, and most importantly, the leaders involved.

A great leader can greatly improve a weak team, but a great team will weaken under a weak leader.

My family and I moved from South Africa to the UK in 2012 to help grow Exceed. In the ten years between 2012 and 2022, there is a decade of memories and milestones. As my younger daughter is fond of saying when she prays before a meal: "Sometimes we have some ups, and sometimes we have some downs!"

"Sometimes we have some ups, and sometimes we have some downs!"

When we arrived in Aberdeen, we were a family of four plus a dog. We are now a family of five plus a very similar looking but different dog. When we arrived, the kids were the ages of two and zero, now they are twelve, ten, and nearly eight! There have been many different moods in our house during that time, but we have become better at maintaining a happy mood. The COVID-19 pandemic tested this to the extreme and we have emerged stronger for it.

The COVID-19 pandemic tested this to the extreme and we have emerged stronger for it.

This reminds me of the helicopter view of a security force (SF) base or an oil rig as we lift off after an intense deployment, or a four-week hitch offshore. For the time that we are deployed, our world consists entirely of what is happening in our immediate vicinity. We live and breathe the immediate eco-system. It is all consuming. It takes all our energy and all of our focus for the duration of our time there. Then as we lift off the helipad or the helideck, we gain perspective; the base or rig appears smaller and smaller until very quickly we realise that the place that contained us for weeks is now a speck on the horizon as we fly away. We are provided with a sense of perspective, and we have a chance to reflect and realise that our time is fleeting, our contribution is our choice, and applying bigger-picture perspective to specific problems is vital.

Our time is fleeting, our contribution is our choice, and applying bigger-picture perspective to specific problems is vital.

Whether an SF base, an offshore rig, or a family home, it can be like a beehive or an anthill: Non-stop activity. And we each have a role to play. We can contribute to creating a better place or we can cause more problems. Our contribution is within our control.

Our contribution is within our control.

My focus from a work perspective has been to contribute to creating the best possible performance-improvement approach to add significant value to upstream frontline teams in the energy sector. This requires an ongoing quest to evolve the service, an ongoing awareness campaign to help organisations understand what is possible, and an ongoing search for the right coaches to lead positive change. Selecting and training potential coaches has seen the evolution of a one-week induction 'sheep-dip'. This course allows us to really get to know potential joiners while allowing them to decide if our culture aligns to their aspirations and purpose.

Setting the right mood for this performance-coach competency programme (PCCP), is something I have had the privilege to master over the last eight years. The first thing that we do on the course is deliberately enable and enhance the three core components of the culture code (Coyle, 2018). We establish purpose, we get vulnerable, we help the group feel psychologically safe. I have found that as course leader, if I go first with the introductions, and I am truly honest about my highs and lows, as well as my fears and failures, it allows everyone else to do the same, and I can see everyone visibly relax. This creates a safe space to truly show up.

We establish purpose, we get vulnerable, we help the group feel psychologically safe.

The PCCP is an incubator for potential. The moodset is protected and controlled throughout the week to allow candidates to express themselves and be themselves. As a result, the feedback we get is that whether-or-not candidates end up working with Exceed, they experience personal growth and a breakthrough in personal confidence. The formula of breaking the ice, breaking down our approach, and then breaking through with a formal presentation and a simulated 'worst-possible' day on task, transforms each candidate from novice to aspirant apprentice in one week.

The formula of breaking the ice, breaking down our approach, and then breaking through with a simulated test, transforms each candidate from novice to aspirant apprentice in one week.

During the recent pandemic, managing our own mood and that of our teams was an immense challenge. However; "The sharpest steel is forged in the hottest fire!" At Exceed we set about surviving the situation to position ourselves for future success.

Our founder is an exceptional leader, especially when the going gets tough. As he navigated a safe course through the crisis, we pivoted to offer virtual support to our clients. An interesting challenge in this context was how to engage and inspire when not physically together in one room. Virtual agendas were curated to enhance the audience experience. These included virtual ice breakers such as laughter therapy, and motivational Q&As with celebrities from international sport and former military. Moodset can be inspired by an injection of "wow" factor in the same way that a game can turn on the introduction of a superstar with 'x' factor.

> *Moodset can be inspired by an injection of "wow"*
> *factor in the same way that a game can turn on*
> *the introduction of a superstar with 'x' factor.*

Collaborating with two former British and Irish Lions captains as well as a commando TV celebrity most definitely inspired my mood and the virtual mood of various workshops.

During the last winter season, I seized an opportunity to coach my son's P5 rugby team at Aberdeen Wanderers. The season culminates with four tournaments in a row. Setting the mood for a group of young players at the threshold of their school sporting careers is a privilege that I do not take lightly. I learned a vital lesson from them about moodset and morale; show you are there and show you really care. Do this by calling their names when they do something right rather than when they do something wrong, and momentum can shift in a momentous way.

> *Do this by calling their names when they do something*
> *right rather than when they do something wrong,*
> *and momentum can shift in a momentous way.*

During lockdown I had the honour of being a guest on *Crux Cast* which is hosted by a friend. He asked for an example of moodset, and I told a story to illustrate: In a few different places around the world, I have been asked to visit multiple rigs for the same operator. Once I flew onto a rig in West Africa in the morning and then a different rig in the afternoon. On the first, crew members avoided eye contact, there were no greetings, doors were closed, and supervisors were sullen. On the second, it was the opposite, personnel were happy and smiling, doors were open, leaders were welcoming.

Same organisation, so in theory same culture, yet the climates on these rigs were at opposite ends of the spectrum. The atmosphere gave away the prevailing mood. One was a place you would not want to be while the other was magnetic and inspired. Setting the mood is a leadership responsibility, we all lead our own mood, we own how we behave.

If I was to define moodset in a simple way, I would say this:

Mood is our inner music, moodset is the playlist that we create and choose!

1

MOODSET

In 2020 I published a book called *Accelerating Automatic*. It draws on my experience as a performance coach with Exceed, a facilitator at Cape Leadership, and before that as a Royal Marines captain. In the book, I unveil a simple model for personal and team mastery. The model integrates mindset, method, and moodset while also unpacking the elements of leadership, teamwork, and discipline.

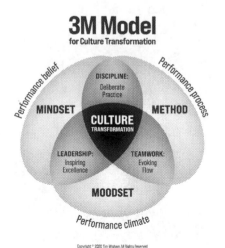

3M Model
for Culture Transformation

Performance belief

Performance process

DISCIPLINE:
Deliberate
Practice

MINDSET

METHOD

CULTURE
TRANSFORMATION

LEADERSHIP:
Inspiring
Excellence

TEAMWORK:
Evoking
Flow

MOODSET

Performance climate

The concept of mood as it contributes to mastery is perhaps the least understood from what I have experienced. For this reason, I have chosen to focus many articles on the topic of mood and to give leaders some valuable insights into how some of the best-known sports coaches and business leaders have created appropriate conditions for excellence.

The language of leading and lagging indicators is partially understood in theory, but the correlation between the two has been an obsession of mine over the last 50,000 hours of my career time as an accountability partner for teams in a variety of different industries—from elite military to upstream energy.

Netflix released a fascinating series called *The Playbook*. I watched every episode in one go. It was like intravenous inspiration for me. The insights from Jose Mourinho and Patrick Mouratoglou were especially intriguing because their guidance influenced some of the most talented and egotistical athletes on the planet. All five of the episodes provide principles for performance from proven practitioners. I was then able to analyse these phenomenal pointers and identify trends while also reflecting on my own playbook for moodset mastery.

Some say that a corporate team is different from a rig team which is different from a sports team. A factory floor is different from a shop floor which is different from a football pitch or a tennis court. But there is a common denominator—people. And to get the best out of people is a craft which requires relentless curiosity and infinite service.

To get the best out of people is a craft which requires relentless curiosity and infinite service.

I am an avid reader, drawn to authors like Simon Sinek, Malcolm Gladwell, and Matthew Syed. These authors are some of the most respected voices when it comes to what it takes to unlock greatness. I learn from them and many others. Their findings often reveal further fascinating ideas about how sustainable progress has been made and what we can learn from societies, communities, and outliers.

Mastering moodset to sustain excellence in a changing world was particularly important during the pandemic when many were working in isolation. As with locker-room inspiration for athletic excellence, the subtle cues for optimal productivity wherever we work are worthy of deliberate focus to achieve measurable progress. It is also important, of course, to celebrate every small success!

TEDx

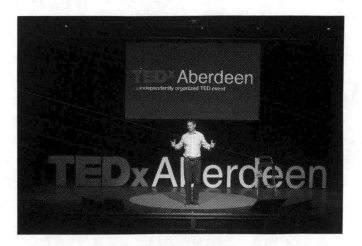

On 31 July 2021, I had the privilege to share an idea with fellow Aberdonians and, via the TEDx platform, with

the world. The essence of the idea is that moodset is as important as mindset.

> *The essence of the idea is that moodset*
> *is as important as mindset.*

Organisational culture can be compared to someone's personality, unlikely to change over a short period of time. Performance climate, however, is like a person's mood; it can be influenced, affected, and changed daily by factors such as leadership, language, and behaviour. Climate takes daily effort and awareness from those in charge.

A big energy company may be known to have a certain culture, but one of their rig teams in the desert or the middle of the ocean will have its own performance climate or mood, its own team atmosphere.

Creating a climate for excellence is like setting an inspired mood. Yet I know from conversations with hundreds of professionals that while mindset or attitude is understood, mood or atmosphere is often ignored.

Leaders need to set the collective mood much like we need to set the collective mind, so it occurred to me that the word 'moodset' should be formalised to help leaders address it as a key leading indicator for campaign success.

> *It occurred to me that the word 'moodset' should*
> *be formalised to help leaders address it as a*
> *key leading indicator for campaign success.*

Moodset is about what we feel and sense, the atmosphere, the energy, the heart, and the soul of a group in a certain place.

A recent study by (Block et al. 2020) Oxford and Birmingham universities proved conclusively that individuals are affected by how others around them are feeling. Mood is contagious.

In other studies (Oswald et al. 2020), researchers have found that happiness makes people around twenty per cent more productive than unhappy workers!

Mood is proven to be contagious, and a positive mood can boost productivity by twenty per cent!

These academic findings align with empirical experience I have had supporting dozens of campaigns where the right performance climate has helped to safely deliver quality results.

> *The right performance climate will*
> *safely deliver quality results.*

Appropriately, the experience of our ten TEDx Aberdeen speakers as a cohort preparing and then delivering our talks benefited from a very special moodset, which was carefully curated and nurtured by several mentors, coaches, and servant-leaders who inspired excellence in us.

My closing line to the audience is a message I am passionate about, and it also represents how we as a cohort felt at the end of the four-month journey involving the application, preparation, and delivery of our ideas from the red spot on the stage at the historical Aberdeen Arts Centre.

"Set your mood to inspired and change your world!"

Mood

A mood board (or inspiration board) is a physical or digital collage of ideas that are commonly used in fields like interior design, fashion, and graphic design. I see close parallels with a vision board.

At TEDx Aberdeen in 2021, I chose to talk about moodset, and I created a storyboard to help me visualise and illustrate the idea I wanted to share. Prior to researching for my talk, I had not come across mood boards, but I love the concept and would add the field of 'talk design' to the common list!

When people ask me what I talked about at TEDx, I say "moodset" and generally get a quizzical look. Let me explain.

Moodset is about what we feel and sense; it is the atmosphere, the energy, the heart and soul of a group in a certain place. It is also referred to as 'performance climate'.

Leaders need to set the collective mood much like we

need to set the collective mind, so it occurred to me that the word 'moodset' should be formalised to help leaders address it as a key leading indicator for purposeful progress to excellence. Moodset is at least as important as mindset for inspiring excellence.

Setting a positive mood can start with some very simple actions—eye contact, a smile, a greeting. Repeated across a team, these simple actions can boost morale and motivate a sense of belonging. Moodset is a key success factor when adversity arrives.

Perhaps if we all make a mood board that inspires us to see others, smile at others, and greet others, we can make our world a little better. Mood for thought?

My TEDx talk on moodset can be viewed on YouTube at this title: Mastering "Moodset" to Improve Team Performance | Tim Wigham | TEDxAberdeen.

Framing

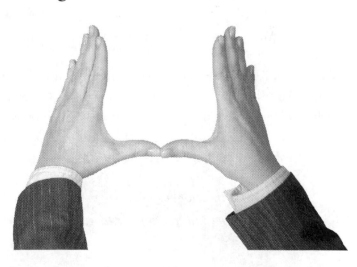

There is so much to learn, yet time can pass us by at a frightening speed!

There is a saying about success being where preparation meets opportunity. There is another about opportunity being disguised as an obstacle.

In December 2021 I had to quarantine at a hotel near Edinburgh Airport due to the COVID-19 Omicron variant.

When I left home in mid-November to travel to Southern Africa for work, quarantine on return was not part of the plan. The Royal Marines call this "dislocation of expectation"!

I quickly realised that how I framed my quarantine would decide whether it was productive time or lost time. I realised that as a performance coach I had an unexpected opportunity to practice positive moodset. I was getting the test whether I was ready or not.

As the sun set on day ten of quarantine, I felt grateful! Grateful for the chance to focus. Grateful for the chance to be still. Grateful for thinking time. Grateful to those who checked in on me. Grateful to those who picked up the slack for me. I had gained perspective about what is important.

Moodset is about creating the conditions to thrive, not just survive. This, of course, requires the right mindset, which is why I believe that where mindset meets moodset there needs to be leadership. In this case I needed to ensure my hotel room allowed me to prioritise.

I believe that where mindset meets
moodset there needs to be leadership.

On reflection, there are three reinforcements I want to share.

Don't just settle for the status quo wherever you are. I ended up moving furniture around in quarantine to be able to stretch and walk around while listening to audiobooks or logging in to virtual workouts. I set up my workspace to be exceptionally efficient. Optimise your environment to the degree that you can. Make sure your productive space is an arena for achievement wherever you are.

Identify inspiring videos to watch and inspiring books to read. With thousands and thousands of drama series and new movies vying for our attention, look for recommendations from respected peers and family. Watch YouTube playlists or TEDx Talks, which teach something useful and light a fire inside. I watched *14 Peaks: Nothing is Impossible* and listened to *High Performance* and *The Ten Pillars of Success*. The fire was burning bright.

Seize the opportunity and do not waste a second. Before we know it, we are back on the hamster wheel. Focus time is incredibly precious. We owe it to our families and to teammates to emerge from any deployment with a renewed sense of purpose and a passion for our priorities.

A moodset for mastery is not standard issue. But it does require high standards. Moodset is led by inspiration, ideally sheep-dip style with surround sound! Finally, seize any and every opportunity to raise the bar for ourselves and, more importantly, for those we serve.

Moodset is led by inspiration, ideally sheep-dip style with surround sound !

Belonging

I listened to the audiobook *Belonging* (Eastwood, 2021). For anyone interested in how to influence a sense of belonging for a particular team or community, this is the best book I have come across.

The author uses the word 'mood' alongside mindset on several occasions. His perspective on how to help teams unlock excellence is built on decades of doing exactly that for international sports teams and organisations. It resonated with my perspective, my purpose, and my aspiration.

One of the teams that Eastwood helped over the last few decades is the South African Protea cricket team. The Proteas were a team of phenomenal players who seldom sustained high performance as a phenomenal team. Eastwood described two retreats he was involved in where extraordinary facilitation created a space for the players to plant the seeds of genuine transformation.

Using his Maori word 'whakapapa' (meaning foundation) to explain, he described how the facilitators helped the team reconnect with their origins, their 'us' story. In South Africa that is a very diverse and difficult history with very different perspectives depending on your ethnicity, religion, and education. Transformation was not going to be easy. But truth and reconciliation had healed a troubled nation in the 1990s, so truth and reconciliation could help a troubled team in the new South Africa.

Two hooks stick with me from his recollection of the retreats.

Firstly, the protea flower – the symbol of the national cricket side – is an incredibly resilient plant. It can withstand the worst conditions such as wind and fire, only to re-emerge more beautiful than before! It is also extremely diverse with hundreds of variations in colour and shape found within the genus. The protea literally represents renewal, transformation, courage, and hope. It is as strong a brand as any sports team could hope to have.

Secondly, ubuntu – meaning 'I am because we are' – was explored and referenced. The epiphany that the team experienced was that the cricket team existed for and from the people of South Africa. More than that, the cricketers wanted the Protea team to be a 'mirror' such that when supporters looked at the team, they saw themselves.

These two ideas are built on a sense of belonging, a sense of where a community comes from, a patriotic pride in the special essence of what makes the team unique.

After both retreats, the Proteas achieved the world number one rank within the next year.

This example is a great reminder that setting the right mood for a world-class team climate, and a world-class team performance, requires deliberate effort and a reconnection with our foundations, our roots, our 'whakapapa'.

A unique identity with a strong sense of history is a great place to start if you want a moodset for mastery.

Forgiving

We recently said goodbye to a true master. A master of moodset. A man like Mandela.

Reading the obituaries was revealing. The Most Reverend Desmond Tutu was much adored and appreciated because of his love and forgiveness.

He led the truth and reconciliation commission and published a book called *No future without forgiveness* about his epiphanies. Tutu is also credited with coining the term 'Rainbow Nation' referring to South Africa's rich tapestry and diversity.

South Africa was on the brink of civil war in the early 1990s. There is no doubt that Tutu played a part alongside Mandela, in transforming the national mood from one of hate to one of hope. Tutu went on to share his learnings and his vision with other troubled regions of the world.

Truth promotes trust. A climate of transparency is a moodset for mastery. As Daniel Coyle reveals in his book *The Culture Code*, a sense of purpose, vulnerability, and psychological safety, is necessary for a true culture of excellence.

Stakeholders need to feel inspired about the meaning of their work, comfortable to share their insights, and secure enough to be honest. This is the essence of what Tutu strove to achieve wherever he went. This is servant leadership.

Every staircase starts with the first step. Archbishop Desmond Tutu taught us that we can all make a difference in our homes and our communities by spreading love rather than hate, and being prepared to forgive to move forward.

Perhaps more so than ever before, the message of truth and reconciliation, of forgiveness and faith, is a significant legacy for us all.

Collaborating

My wife loves conquering puzzles. She loves the sense of accomplishment that comes with successful completion. She starts and then the family gets involved as progress is made. Sound familiar?

The puzzles we complete provide a brilliant metaphor.

My wife typically gets the puzzle and boldly makes a start. The rest of the family is invited to get involved but only if we want. Initially the challenge looks like an impossible task. The pieces are difficult to link to the picture, and there are 1,000 of them so it is easy to find an excuse to do something else!

After a day, the boundary frame has been completed by the 'project leader' so the family starts to believe it might be possible to get this puzzle done. We all begin to offer a little more time and interest to the campaign. We all start following, if only out of curiosity.

Then by day three, the picture takes on a life of its own. Everyone in the family is drawn in. No one wants to miss out on the final push to the finish line. It becomes 'our' puzzle and 'our' success. Finding the right place for each piece is still difficult but the mood is now set; one team, one mission.

When the final puzzle piece is placed, there is excited celebration. It is considered a team effort even though there is a clear leader and a few 'first followers'. It is another reference point for the concept of 'play' as I described in my TEDx talk on moodset.

On any campaign, if team players enjoy playing, and they feel their contribution makes a difference, the seemingly impossible can be accomplished!

It starts with leadership, it flows with shared ownership, it ends with a mini championship.

It starts with leadership, it flows with shared ownership, it ends with a mini championship.

Embracing a challenge builds character and collaboration. Enrolment, and encouragement is part of that challenge. Celebration is the easy part once the challenge is overcome.

Music

Most of us can relate to the initiation of Christmas soundtracks as background music to get us in the mood for Christmas from early December. The music reminds us of the energy and enthusiasm associated with that time of year, and it eases us into the celebrations and congregations that we enjoy at Christmas time.

When I am preparing to workout at home, I have certain soundtracks which get me in the mood for a tough gym session. It is different to the Christmas soundtrack, but it is appropriate for the task at hand!

In the car, I typically listen to audiobooks although if I am driving to the gym or to a physical challenge, I might listen to energising music to get me in the mood.

On Spotify, I have created a playlist called 'Memory Lane' which is a chronology of my favourite tunes from each year going back to the 1980s. Each song has a specific set of memories associated and it can transport me back in time! The playlist lifts my spirit.

I recently read an article about power songs: The creation of a personal power song which integrates affirmation, motivation, and confidence. It is a song you create (in other words write the lyrics) and then work with a musician to fine tune!

The point is that moodset is all about the background music, literally and figuratively. It is within our control in our own environment, to create a climate for optimal energy; an atmosphere which suits the occasion, the task, or the challenge.

If you are a team leader, think about the background music for your team (figuratively speaking). Is the team 'hearing' something that lifts the mood, or is there the sound of silence? Are they excited by the soundtrack, or depressed by the drumbeat?

> *If you are a team leader, think about the background music for your team.*

Creating a climate for individual and team excellence is like setting the right mood. Climate is like the background music. Get it right and anything is possible. Get it wrong and very little gets done.

Turnaround

When I was preparing for my TEDx talk last year, one of the aspects of team performance that grabbed my attention was the turnaround team-talk, or the trigger for a fightback. The pre-game or half-time team talk from the coach or captain that changed the course of the game or inspired a level of commitment that was almost gladiatorial.

There were some games that immediately sprang to mind; 'The Miracle of Istanbul', when Steven Gerrard led Liverpool to an unbelievable Champions League fightback victory in 2005. Scotland coming from 31 points down against England at Twickenham in 2019 to draw 38-38 and retain the Calcutta Cup. Or the New England Patriots reversing a 28-3 deficit to win Super Bowl LI in 2017!

Djibrul Cisse who played for Liverpool in that miraculous fightback of 2005 described their turnaround; "Stevie gets up (at half time) and says that Liverpool is all he has, it is his club, all he has ever known, and he does not want to be the laughingstock of the history of the Champions League." The Frenchman added: " ...that half time speech will remain imprinted in my mind forever."

> *"That half time speech will remain*
> *imprinted in my mind forever."*

Gerrard then scored the first goal in the fightback within 10 minutes of the start of the second half. He backed up his fighting talk with an inspirational header to score the first goal for his side. The rest is history as Liverpool went on to stun AC Milan and win on penalties after extra time.

At Twickenham in 2019, England were 31 points ahead at their traditional fortress 'HQ'. Somehow, 'Scotland-the-Brave' fought back to 38-31 ahead, with minutes to go. The Guardian described it as perhaps the most remarkable comeback in Six Nations history. England managed to score in the dying minutes and tie the game, but Scotland retained the cup.

> *"Perhaps the most remarkable comeback*
> *in Six Nations history!"*

Various reports described a heated halftime exchange between coach Gregor Townsend and pivot Finn Russell. Russell apparently refused to kick anymore, and he came out to inspire the incredible fightback with a phenomenal 'man-of-the-match' performance which included intercepts and passing skills that almost defied belief! It would not be an exaggeration to say he was instrumental in every score of the second half.

In Super Bowl LI, Tom Brady suddenly fired into life in the second half to produce a performance that will go into National Football League folklore. He inspired a comeback which has been described as one of the greatest of all time.

A reporter noted, "It's said a team takes on the identity of its leader in times of adversity, and that's about the best explanation possible for the New England Patriots beating the Atlanta Falcons 34-28 in overtime for the greatest Super Bowl comeback ever."

*"It's said a team takes on the identity of
its leader in times of adversity."*

During 2021 I watched *Chasing the Sun* which is a documentary about the Springboks winning the 2019 Rugby World Cup in Japan. This behind-the-scenes documentary was incredibly inspiring.

Rassie Erasmus was the Springboks coach while Siya Kolisi was the captain.

Kolisi was asked what Rassie had said or done to inspire such a phenomenal turnaround by the Springboks (between 2017 and 2019). He said the coach had turned the players' focus away from themselves, and towards the millions of South Africans who were desperate for hope.

Rassie had helped them realise that they had a chance to transform a nation. He turned perceived pressure into real purpose. This united the entire squad behind a true sense of destiny. The appointment of Kolisi as captain was also a well-deserved master stroke.

Before the RWC final against England, Rassie reminded the Boks that the game was no longer about them. It was much bigger. The Springboks won the game 32-12.

> *"The game was no longer about*
> *them. It was much bigger."*

In all these examples, there was a catalyst for the turnaround or the transformation. Someone or something triggered a fightback or a fearless focus which changed the course of a game or a team. Often it is a talismanic figure who walks the talk and ignites the fightback.

The mood of these teams went from hopeless to hopeful to inspirational. Often it just takes a spark to start a fire, but many teams wait for someone else to light the match. Why wait? Why not be the spark for your team?

> *"Why not be the spark for your team?"*

Language

Language plays a massive role in the subtleties of moodset. Actual language and body language.

I listened to *Game Changers* by Dave Asprey. In an early chapter, he references four words that create a negative mood for the speaker, and the listener. The four 'weasel' words as he references them are 'can't', 'need', 'try', and 'bad'.

Note your own resistance to this list as you read the four words. Note how we justify using them. Now reconsider with an open mind how these words might limit us and/or our teams.

Performance climate is highly dependent on leadership cues such as behaviour and language. Another way of explaining this is body language and actual language.

In body language I will include facial expressions which apply in the virtual world as well. So, start with a smile, accompanied by a greeting!

It is amazing how many barriers this combination can break. My good friend Eric Doyle who started a weekly LinkedIn show called the *Big Live Breakfast Burrito*, always reminds the audience that the 'price of entry' is a simple greeting and an introduction. Simple but so significant to setting the scene for support and sociability.

Eye contact and intentional attention also sends a strong signal to others that we are present, respectful, and purposeful. The opposite behaviour includes people who do not make eye contact, and who are always distracted. Does that sound inspiring?

Using people's names is a great way to create a positive connection where possible, and the virtual world even helps us out with this so there is no excuse! But in face-to-face environments, learning names can be a game-changer for moodset. A two-way greeting by name in a team environment is a 'norm' or 'cue' which signifies a culture of respect.

A two-way greeting by name in a team environment is a 'norm' or 'cue' which signifies a culture of respect.

The language of blame is possibly the most limiting cue a leader can use. Nothing erodes a performance climate like "It was their fault", or "It is not my job". This language is often accompanied by body language and facial expressions which even from a distance can tell a viewer that the huddle is complaining and blaming. You can visualise what I mean.

The positive alternative which we should all aspire to, is a 'huddle for good'. A group conversation which exudes energy and has nothing to hide.

These subtle but powerful cues ultimately set the stage and the state for performance. Whether we are talking about a family or a community, a team or a tribe, language is a leading indicator of how limited (or otherwise) collective success will be.

Much has been written about the language we use. When I completed my professional coaching course, one of my prescribed books was *You are What you Say* by Larry Rothstein and Matthew Budd. In this excellent book, Dr Budd explains that our words play a major role in determining, not just reflecting, our health and well-being. He explores how the body 'learns' many of its reactions, consciously and unconsciously, through language.

In my view, the language that we use as leaders, also influences the team dynamic and human behaviour. Workers and followers conform to the subtle cues of their management. Our words play a major role in team health and team well-being.

Two words that can have a disproportionately negative impact on morale and performance are 'I' and 'they'. Thankfully, a word that can undo that damage, if adopted as a better replacement, is 'we'.

All too often I have experienced the disappointment of hearing "I will decide" when it should be a team decision, or "they messed up" when in fact we were all involved somehow. Incredibly, very little is lost but a huge amount is gained if instead the message is "we messed up, and we will decide how to improve together".

I have been on so many projects where the ubiquitous 'they' are to blame, that I wonder if 'they' have ever done anything right!

How about a switch to a world where the only time we use I or they is to say, "I made a mistake", or "they did an excellent job". Otherwise use 'we' to include team and togetherness.

Based on the 'we' cultures I've been privileged to serve, we'll be amazed at the positive impact on morale and performance that this subtle shift can have.

Behaviour

I have become intrigued by kindness.

Kindness was not something I used to ponder often. Now I place it in my top five values alongside respect and courage.

"Kindness is the language which the deaf can hear and the blind can see."

It really is so important and so simple, yet apparently not so easy for many.

Random acts of kindness (RAK) are particularly inspiring. I am no 'RAK guru' but I was recently involved in a very small initiative which surprised me: My birthday was approaching, and Facebook suggested I raise money for a cause as part of my birthday focus. I spontaneously decided to go for it but set a modest target as I was conscious that people are being asked for money all the time.

Well before my age increased, several friends had seemingly randomly donated way more than the target I'd set. One, just looked at the target shortfall and covered it. I've not seen him since 2011! This kindness is touching, unsolicited, and completely unselfish. It reminds me of the concept of 'pay it forward'.

Pay it forward is best illustrated for me by parenting. I can never directly repay my parents for their kindness when I was growing up, but I can be kind to my children as they grow up. I try to remind myself of that when the kids are testing my patience. It enhances my own awareness of how much my parents did for me.

Interestingly with parenting, sometimes we must be 'cruel to be kind', such as limiting the amount of ice cream my seven-year-old consumes in a day!

There is a lot of negativity around. Would it not be great to reduce that?

It starts with each of us, and each of our daily interactions with others. Small opportunities which if seized by everyone, could make a massive difference in the world. How hard is it to just be kind?

Here are three very simple acts of kindness that I try to maintain:

- Greet others.
- Smile more.
- Listen to understand.

And finally, some notable quotes to inspire us on the subject:

"My religion is very simple. My religion is kindness."

— Dalai Lama

"Kind words can be short and easy to speak, but their echoes are truly endless."

— Mother Teresa

Inspiration

'Everyone loves an underdog.' The *Rocky* story appeals to everyone because we all face adversity at some time or another and we seek inspiration to turn things around and to triumph against the odds.

All champions have had to fight through personal or public doubt. The few minutes of podium glory are built on years of sacrifice and hard work.

The *Rocky* film series was inspired by a real boxer. A relative unknown who went nearly fifteen rounds with the great Muhammad Ali.

Project teams are made up of many inexperienced and often unknown personnel. Teams are required to step into the proverbial ring and take on whatever challenges are thrown at them.

To become a champion team means that ordinary people need to achieve the extraordinary, together. Many teams fail just like many underdogs merely make up the numbers. So, what is the most important lesson we can learn from *Rocky* when it comes to reaching the top of the steps?

For me the answer must be desire - a burning, inextinguishable desire to prove what is possible when you set your mind to it. Achieving collective desire in a new project team requires careful leadership and organisation. We call it 'one team, one mission' and have an initial step in our Exceed approach which focuses on building team identity and inducting project members into the fold.

I'm reminded of one of my favourite quotes from Mark Twain: "It's not the size of the dog in the fight, it's the size of the fight in the dog." The underdog with the inextinguishable desire to fight through adversity and emerge unconquered at the top of the steps. Thanks for the inspiration, *Rocky*.

After eight years in the Royal Marines, I moved to Cape Town to study an MBA. Being an avid rugby supporter,

I was excited to watch the Boks take on the All Blacks that year at Newlands. The evening before the test match I bumped into Joost van der Westhuizen by chance. He had always been an inspiring and electric player to watch, and I'd listed him along with Nelson Mandela as a legendary South African I would personally love to meet.

Joost went on to play 89 tests for the Boks, he led the team and led the most tries by a Bok for a long time before Bryan Habana eventually overtook him. He was and always will be a hero of South African rugby.

In 2010 Joost was diagnosed with motor neurone disease (MND). Instead of wallowing in self-pity he faced this monster the same way he'd faced down Jonah Lomu in the 1995 RWC final. He championed a foundation to raise money for research to help defeat this terrible disease.

Joost faced many setbacks in his life, but he never ever quit. I'm grateful I got to meet him, and I find his courage in the face of harrowing adversity to be one of the most inspiring reference points imaginable. He died aged forty-five and will be remembered for his indomitable warrior mindset, his unselfish fight for those who may suffer his fate with MND, and his dignity in death.

Reference points for inspiration need to be personal and meaningful. They give us role models, they help bring perspective, and they remind us that what has been done before can be done again.

Don't quit, don't wait, joost do it!

An excellent quote recently caught my eye: "Managers light a fire under you, leaders light a fire within you."

The speaker, Les Brown emphasises the importance of manifesting your dreams. He inspires, motivates, and persuades using personal anecdotes and professional learning to emphasise the following points:

- It's possible (to achieve your dream).
- It's necessary (to pursue your dream).
- It's worth it (in the end, no matter the sacrifice, if you are being true to yourself and doing what you are passionate about).

To create a spark, we need friction and traction - we need energy and synergy. When I was looking at my options beyond military life, I identified the MBA as an excellent catalyst for my professional journey, a way of harnessing my transferable skills and channelling them to create value in the commercial world. It was only when I took action to visit the Graduate School of Business in Cape Town and invest in the application process that my fire was fuelled and there was no turning back.

Beyond business school, one of the tools that helped me crystalise my thinking about why and how I wanted to do what I wanted to do, was the book *What Colour is Your Parachute* by Richard Nelson Bolles. This book takes a structured approach to helping you figure out your future and emphasises the importance of pursuing what you are considered an expert at as well as what you really enjoy doing. Often those two answers coincide.

In *Good to Great* by Jim Collins, he talks about the Hedgehog Concept: Three overlapping circles: What lights your fire ('passion')? What could you be best in the world at ('best at')? What makes you money ('economic engine')?

Common to most respected guidance on the matter of creating value and achieving success is the key question of what are you passionate about, what do you enjoy doing, what lights your fire? If you can honestly figure that out and find work which allows you to express your passion, you are in the top twenty percent of world workers according to various *Gallup* workplace engagement surveys.

It is never too late to confirm what lights your fire but don't leave it too late to ignite the flame.

I finally read *The Alchemist* by Paulo Coelho.

The word alchemist comes from alchemy, which has origins in the Greek word khemeia, meaning 'art of transmuting metals.' 'Active since ancient times, alchemists could be considered very early chemists because of their work trying to transform base metals into gold.'

In this classic story, the central figure represents all of us: He goes in search of life's treasure and along the way gets lessons in meaning from various mentors and experiences.

Resounding themes for me were the following.

1. Follow your dream.

    There is a great quote in the book: "When you want something, all the universe conspires in helping you to achieve it."

    Conor McGregor the 'notorious' MMA fighter has a great perspective on this. "If you can see it here, and you have the courage enough to speak it, it will happen."

    Santiago, the boy in the book, dreams of treasure at the pyramids. Despite never having seen the pyramids, he pursues the dream and completes an incredible journey to get there, and back. He seeks and finds his own 'personal legend' – his sense of purpose.

2. Listen to your heart.

    In *The Alchemist* there is a central theme summed up by this quote; "Listen to your heart. It knows all things, because it came from the soul of the world, and it will one day return there."

    Your heart will guide you to your treasure. 'Head' decisions tend to be influenced by prevailing commentary and culture. Heart decisions tend to tie into what you know is the right thing to do, for you, and for the world. I view this as mindset vs moodset, or head vs heart.

    That nagging gut feeling, or intuition is your heart trying to get your attention.

    Oprah Winfrey said, "I've trusted the still, small voice of intuition my entire life. And the only time I've made mistakes is when I didn't listen."

3. Believe in yourself.

    The Alchemist provides this classic: "But if you believe yourself worthy of the thing you fought so hard to get, then you become an instrument of God, you help the soul of the world, and you understand why you are here."

    Being authentic and striving to be the best version of ourselves is intuitively obvious, yet we get distracted by innumerable external factors which sow the seeds of doubt.

Paulo Coelho himself is the best example of this point. His book *The Alchemist* initially did not sell, it was considered a flop. However, he persevered. He believed there was a reason his heart had told him to write it.

Today, *The Alchemist* has sold sixty-five million copies and been on The New York Times bestseller list for more than six years. It has also been translated into eighty different languages, setting the Guinness World Record for the most translated book by any living author.

In summary, this allegory about a young shepherd in search of his treasure, about finding the gold in ourselves, is a bestseller because achieving alchemy is possible.

For me, there is nothing like a truly outstanding movie to inspire imagination and awe!

The Greatest Showman, was right up there with the most inspiring movies I have ever seen. I watched it for a second time and could literally feel my emotions 'roller-coasting' as the story unfolded.

Interestingly, I am not normally into musicals, but this was a massive exception. Below are two of the song titles, and some lyrics with relevant meaning, for achieving a positive breakthrough in life.

1. 'The Greatest Show'.

    Some lyrics: "Your fever dream, can't you see it getting closer, just surrender 'cause you feel the feeling taking over, it's fire, it's freedom, it's flooding open ..."

    Dream it, believe it, speak it, execute it. Your life can be your own greatest show.

As my good friend and serial entrepreneur – Dom Moorhouse – often says: "The person with the most stories, wins!"

2. 'This is Me'.

Some lyrics: "I am brave, I am bruised, I am who I'm meant to be, this is me. Look out 'cause here I come, and I'm marching on to the beat I drum; I'm not scared to be seen, I make no apologies, this is me."

We all have a gift. We all have something to offer. Be the best version of you that you can be. Fail, but learn. Stay true to who you are and who you believe you can be.

As Marianne Williamson said, "As we let our own light shine, we unconsciously give others permission to do the same."

This movie was inspired by a true story. No doubt it was dramatised to some degree, but the positive lessons were clear to me: Don't settle for less than you deserve, and be authentic to unleash your true potential, which in turn will unleash the potential of others.

> *Don't settle for less than you deserve, and be*
> *authentic to unleash your true potential, which*
> *in turn will unleash the potential of others.*

Enjoy your show!

The Springboks won the 2019 Rugby World Cup in Japan.

I am an avid Springbok fan but also a passionate performance coach, so my reflections have drawn on the inspiration I felt during and after that final as all the dots joined up looking back.

I think the key difference between the two sides contesting the final, was that it subsequently became clear the Boks were playing for something much, much bigger than a trophy. They had a purpose which transcended rugby, it was about uniting a troubled land and inspiring the next generation. Not only that, but key stakeholders within the squad have also emerged from poverty to prove that anything is possible if you believe, and you put in the work.

When Rassie Erasmus was interviewed after accepting 'Best Coach' at the International rugby awards, he humbly cited three excellent points when asked how his team had won.

1. Belief.

   Belief in better, belief in each other, belief in what is possible. James Haskell summed it up perfectly in one of his vlogs: "Two years ago, South Africa couldn't win a raffle, now they have won the World Cup!" Rassie, Siya, and indeed the entire squad had to believe that despite some very poor results in 2017, 'Big in Japan' could be done.

2. Luck.

   This is outside a team's control, so it is not a sound strategy to rely on luck, however, when it goes your way, your belief builds from possible to probable. New Zealand faced England in the first semi-final. It was an enormous game which did two things, it knocked out the defending champions, and it created unprecedented hype around the favoured England team. Outside Bok control, but another stroke of luck for a team quietly on the rise.

3. Destiny.

Destiny is what is meant to be, what is written in the stars, your inescapable fate. There's no avoiding destiny — it's going to happen no matter what you do. One can't help feeling that the sequel to *Invictus* has now received its script, with the star being Siya Kolisi. The story could not be more inspiring: A black South African, born as Mandela was uniting a nation, learning to play rugby in a deprived area with little support, but who against all odds went on to captain the Springboks! It is the stuff of legend. Quite frankly, England did not stand a chance against this sense of destiny.

So, what can ordinary leaders and teams take from this extraordinary tale? In a word, 'inspiration'. But we all know that before the inspiration comes a lot of perspiration. Belief grows when you are perspiring for a purpose which has real meaning (to all involved). Subordinate to that of course, there needs to be exceptional talent and an outstanding training system, but history is littered with examples of wasted talent due to a lack of meaning, or a weak sense of collective purpose.

Bottom line, you need 'buy in', you need belief, you need a sense of destiny.

Kolisi was recently asked what Rassie had said or done to inspire such a phenomenal turnaround by the Springboks. He said the coach had turned the players' focus away from themselves, and towards the millions of South Africans who were desperate for hope. Rassie had helped them realise that they had a chance to transform a nation. He turned perceived pressure into real purpose. This united the entire squad behind a true sense of destiny. The appointment of Kolisi as captain was a well-deserved master stroke. The whole country started to believe.

If you believe in destiny, you create your own luck.

Friday Night Lights provides wholesome TV viewing. I watched all five series and want to highlight some of the classic performance lessons scripted in. For anyone interested in winning, there is plenty of inspiration.

1. Mindset.

    Winning the state championship is the ultimate dream for the players. There is a scene in one of the episodes when Coach Taylor simply writes 'STATE' on the whiteboard. Nothing needs to be said, nothing else needs to be written. The mentality is clear – we are going for STATE – that is the unifying mission, and it drives the method which now has an end in mind.

2. Method.

    Discipline and teamwork. This applied as much to the coaching group as to the player group. Strategy for the season and tactics for each game. Planning meetings to get to agreement and alignment. Video analysis and performance review. In addition, a clear and critical aspect of the method that Coach Taylor used to get results, was his personal interest and personal relationship with each of the leaders in the team. He invested time, energy, and effort in mentoring his key players. It was deliberate, and it was a differentiator.

3. Moodset.

Zero tolerance for prima donnas and egomaniacs. No one was allowed to be bigger than the team. Coach Taylor created a climate for excellence. When he was unfairly ousted from his position coaching the Dillon Panthers, he moved across to coach the East Dillon Lions who were in complete disarray. Over a short time, he led the prevailing mood from despair to hope. He created an atmosphere of belief. Most of the players remained the same but the mood changed and then so did the results. The players he did bring across were servant leaders who enhanced the mood. Clear eyes, full hearts – can't lose.

Most of the players remained the same but the mood changed and then so did the results.

This fictional story of a town in Texas with two schools and their respective football teams is just a story. But life is all about stories and stories can inspire us to be more, and to achieve more. I recommend this series to coaches, leaders, and indeed to any team seeking success.

Bohemian Rhapsody; what a great movie!

Of course, it helped in my case, to have grown up with Queen soundtracks reverberating around the place: There is a sentimental attachment to the songs and indeed nostalgia is generated on hearing much of their music.

A behind-the-scenes insight into the life of Freddie Mercury is also fascinating. I was reminded of the importance of seeking first to understand, before making assumptions about people.

Many of the Queen song-lyrics represent the emotional challenges this lead singer was wrestling with on life's journey. And when he died, he was only forty-five years old! So much achieved in such a short lifespan.

What inspired me most was the final chapter of the movie when Freddie Mercury embraced the people in his circle who genuinely cared. He realised his true purpose which was so much bigger than him, and he chose to perform onstage for Live-Aid at Wembley Stadium despite having recently been diagnosed with HIV Aids.

Queen was the catalyst to get the phones ringing to exceed Bob Geldof's one-million-pound target. Freddie Mercury gave the performance of his life when he stood to earn no money, and when he was most vulnerable.

The Show Must Go On has always been one of my all-time favourite songs. Now it has new meaning.

Life moves fast. It is important that we maintain perspective.

Nothing inspires perspective like the sudden loss of a close friend or family member. I have been affected by both in the last ten years, so I've experienced the sudden crystal clarity about what really matters versus what seems to matter when hypnotised by the merry-go-round of life.

As a former Royal Marine, I maintain a close interest in military operations and of course tracked the interventions in Iraq and Afghanistan, as well as the casualties of those campaigns. Many lost their lives and many also lost their limbs. These survivors who had to learn to process what happened while also learning to function hour to hour, day to day with new disabilities, provide all the inspiration we should need to act on our perspective.

> *"Your heart is free, have the courage*
> *to follow it." – Braveheart*

Watch the Invictus Games and you'll understand heart. What is interesting is that it seems that often we need a life-changing event to break us out of our hypnosis. We can easily fall into the trap of sleepwalking through life, rather than spreading our wings and lifting off.

Follow your heart, pursue your passion, be present and create value.

> *"Intuition is the whisper of the*
> *soul." – Jiddu Krishnamurti*

All the people I respect the most, regularly say; "I have learned more and more, to listen to my gut. When I have ignored my intuition, I have always regretted it."

Our unconquerable souls seek the freedom to express all that we are, and all that we can be. Free from self-limiting beliefs and small-minded judgement.

Leave a legacy by being everything you could have been. Follow your heart and trust your soul. Be deliberate and be present.

> *"Put your heart, mind, and soul into*
> *even your smallest acts. This is the secret*
> *of success." Swami Sivananda*

2

CLIMATE

In my 2021 TEDx Talk, I discussed family climate as well as workplace climate. One of the activities we do with family is car travel. I stated the following: "Creating a climate in the car that improves the mood of the majority, helps the journey, and gets us happier to the destination."

> *"Creating a climate in the car that improves the mood of the majority, helps the journey, and gets us happier to the destination."*

Journey

The Wigham family was on holiday in South Africa in 2022. We took a long drive as we traversed the Garden Route of the Western Cape from Cape Town to Sedgefield. There were five of us in a small car and it was thirty-nine degrees outside! The journey could have been a pressure cooker, however, the car had excellent air conditioning which ultimately kept us cool.

This got me thinking about climate control, whether air conditioning or central heating, and how analogous it is to leadership, teamwork, and moodset.

Optimising a team performance climate requires attention to detail – social detail. These details include cues and clues about team dynamics, team welfare, and team unity. In the heat of battle, we need our emotions to be cool so that we can maintain composure and collaborate as one.

There is an optimal temperature for human performance in any context. That temperature range is critical, and leaders need to use the metaphorical thermometer and thermostat to sustain the right conditions for excellence.

Wikipedia describes a thermostat as a regulating device component which senses the temperature of a physical system and performs actions so that the system's temperature is maintained near a desired setpoint.

This is very similar to setting collective human emotion at the right point most of the time.

For leaders, this involves a lot of situational awareness and a lot of listening. It requires empathy as well as energy. It requires treating others as they would like to be treated.

On our holiday drive, the temperature outside was very hot, but the journey was cool. Everyone in the car had a voice, everyone had equal influence on the air conditioning. Everyone was expected to contribute to climate control. The journey was (mostly) fun!

Assessment

In 2016 I spent several months in Saudi Arabia. Exceed Performance had agreed to conduct five performance climate assessments of five different land rigs in the desert.

It was an interesting experience, and I learned a lot. The biggest takeaway after so many visits and interviews with supervisors at each rig, was that my first impression, which was typically formed within the first five minutes of my arrival, was reinforced and proven correct over the ensuing three days.

I became highly attuned to the prevailing atmosphere. Certain cues and clues told a story as I scanned the scene and signed in.

Certain cues and clues tell a story as we scan
a new scene and sign into a new place.

We are all sensitive to signals and situations. We all form an impression of the prevailing atmosphere wherever we go. We develop this skill from a very young age.

There is 'no second chance at a first impression'. I was given this wise advice a long time ago and I remind myself and my kids of this on a regular basis.

There is no second chance at a first impression.

What are some of the components of the impression we make on others? How can we behave to be our best selves and to enhance how others experience us? Here are some ideas based on my observations.

- Be polite.
- Be punctual.
- Be purposeful.
- Be positive.
- Be prepared.

The great thing about this list is that these points are largely within our control.

I have facilitated dozens of virtual workshops and I consider my most important role to be to delicately craft a professional moodset for the duration of the session.

Through careful and deliberate preparation, my aim is to keep the agenda focused and on time, to maintain a positive atmosphere, and to ensure that presenters, group leaders, and all attendees are prepared in advance.

We all have an opportunity to positively contribute to the prevailing atmosphere. I remind myself of this whenever the surrounding energy level is in decline. Sounds simple, not always easy.

We can start by building better awareness of the atmosphere where we are!

Adjustment

I have worked on dozens of offshore rigs, but it had been a while since the last time I was offshore.

Inevitably there is a sense of uncertainty and anxiety when

returning to a less familiar environment. This would apply to anyone who has been away from the frontline for a period, and, definitely to anyone who is brand new to a place of work.

So, what helps with that feeling of acceptance and belonging from when we are in the helicopter, to when we land on the helideck, to then when we receive an induction into an unfamiliar place?

It always starts with leadership. A big indicator is whether the key leaders of operations and the installation, take the time to meet you at the 'door', or in the case of a rig, in the heli-lounge. On a rig, these leaders are the Drilling Supervisor (DSV) and the Offshore Installation Manager (OIM).

When I arrived offshore recently, the DSV and OIM could not have been more welcoming. Not only had they taken the time to greet and brief us, but they did it with a smile on their faces and with eye contact to each of the apprehensive arrivals. The body language was open, and the proverbial office-door was offered open. It was a purposeful introduction.

After a walkaround and a show-around, we were ushered to the end of our tour to ensure that we could get dinner before it finished. This showed empathy and care.

Over the next few days there were a few indicators which provided real insight into the prevailing culture code.

1. First, the OIM thanked the crew for the collective effort which had helped achieve three years without a lost-time incident (LTI). This cemented my sense of physical and psychological safety. This team clearly looked after each other and their legacy.

2. Second, the DSV showed self-effacing vulnerability by admitting he is bad at remembering names (as am

I). He went around the room listening to input from everyone present and thanking us for the input.

In his book *The Culture Code*, Daniel Coyle described his findings from half a decade of research and explained that the top three ingredients for a high-performing culture are purpose, psychological safety, and vulnerability.

I was sure, there offshore, that these three elements were present in abundance which is why I felt a sense of belonging and a sense of belief in the potential for all cultures to build towards a better performance climate.

If the indicators and components described here are given the attention they deserve, a professional 'family' atmosphere is sure to follow.

Hope

Fear is a fascinating topic. Psychology Today describes fear thus: "There are many things that motivate us. But the most powerful motivator of all is fear. Fear is a primal instinct that served us as cave dwellers and still serves us today. It keeps us alive, because if we survive a bad experience, we never forget how to avoid it in the future."

But as the author of that article explained, <u>fear is a negative motivator</u>.

Goodreads provides a quote from Jon Meacham: "The opposite of fear is hope, defined as the expectation of good fortune not only for us but for a group to which we belong. Fear feeds anxiety and produces anger. Hope, particularly in a political sense, breeds optimism and feelings of well-being. Fear pushes away; hope pulls others closer."

Hope breeds feelings of well-being.
Hope pulls others closer.

At a macro level we have an intriguing comparison of how leaders can create moodset. President Putin of Russia is using force and fear to intimidate and threaten Ukraine and NATO. President Zelensky is using hope and confidence to inspire a mood of optimism despite the overwhelming odds facing Ukraine.

Zelensky is being rightly praised for his courage in the face of adversity. Rather than flee like the leader of Afghanistan when the Taliban came to town, Zelensky seems to be defying Goliath and rallying the citizens of Kyiv and beyond, to stand and fight rather than to give up. More than that, he is inspiring people around the world to stand up for human rights and to defend democracy against oppressive tyranny.

Hope will always trump fear, because striving for the

light is more inspiring than avoiding the dark. Donald Trump's slogan when he ran for election in 2016 was, "Make America great again!" The positive spin attracted voters who believed that the future could be brighter than the present.

COVID 19 cast a huge shadow over all of us for several years. Early pictures of dead bodies piling up in the streets of many cities, spread fear across the globe. The virus threatened to change our way of life forever. Then came hope, hope of a vaccine, hope for immunity, and hope for a way of living with the virus much like we do with other diseases.

In my TEDx talk I referenced South Africa. The country of my birth, and a place where fear abounded before Nelson Mandela helped inspire hope by painting a different picture of how the future could be. A future that allowed everyone equal opportunity to flourish.

The first black Springbok captain, Siya Kolisi, led South Africa to victory at the 2019 RWC. He is the very embodiment of the brighter future Mandela described, and Kolisi voiced his own hope which is that his country might harmonise after seeing what is possible when diverse individuals unite behind a righteous cause for good.

Dan Carter, one of the greatest rugby players ever, described the paralysis of fear if outcomes became the focus. He reflected on what hope can achieve if players remain humble, hungry, and focused only on the process. Do the right thing, at the right time, for the right reason. He was player of the RWC final won by the All Blacks in 2015.

Do the right thing, at the right
time, for the right reason.

The obvious example of facing fear is David against Goliath. A young boy against a giant warrior. The difference? David had hope through faith, Goliath was used to instilling fear through physical and verbal intimidation. The outcome of that confrontation is either inspiring, or a cautionary tale depending on our perspective.

In every example, hope went hand-in-hand with massive action too. Motivation starts with movement. Take deliberate action.

At a personal level, I aspire to believe in better. Hope is more inspiring than fear so I will face fear with hope and a belief that justice and excellence will prevail. As Abraham Lincoln said, "I will study and prepare myself, and someday my chance will come."

"I will study and prepare myself, and
someday my chance will come."

Environment

Environment is a fundamental component of moodset. Managing our surroundings can make a significant difference. The dictionary defines environment thus, the surroundings or conditions in which a person, animal, or plant lives or operates.

I was discussing surroundings with a colleague on a rig offshore. The food was excellent on this rig, so sitting and chatting in the galley was a highlight of the day!

The surroundings in the galley were not conducive to eating completely clean, if that was our intent. The food was delicious, plentiful, and there were a multitude of options (including many healthy ones).

Then there was a fridge full of delectable looking desserts – these were visible through a glass door. In addition, the tuck shop opens during dinner, and sells treats such as chocolates, crisps, and sodas.

Clearly it is our choice whether we eat too much, eat a

dessert, and/or buy chocolate from the shop, but as the likes of *Weight Watchers* would tell us, one of the best ways to stick to a way of eating, is to remove temptation and manage our surroundings.

Remove temptation and manage our surroundings.

Back home onshore I try to manage the domestic environment to support my aspirations for eating healthy meals and snacks more than the alternative! This involves having cheese, nuts, and dark chocolate more available than biscuits, crisps, and assorted candy.

Creating an environment that (only) offers better choices will guarantee better results.

Around the time that I was offshore, it was the annual CrossFit open in which I compete every year.

The rig I was on had a superb offshore gym, but it is not designed to be a standard CrossFit Box. The announced workout was straight forward but still required tape on the floor, a wall, a dumbbell of a certain weight, and a box of a certain height.

The rig itself was a Semi-Submersible which meant a degree of pitch and roll; interesting dynamic when negotiating a box jump!

I managed to find a time the gym was quiet and managed to set up the area to do the workout (WOD). The dumbbell was heavier and the box less stable than it should have been. However, I was happy that I managed to video the workout as required and to record a score which would count.

For the next two WODs I was able to go into the Box

at CrossFit Aberdeen onshore. Clearly the environment within CFA is optimal for completing a prescribed Open WOD, and on both occasions I was able to draw energy from coaches and comrades watching on.

The difference in my relative CrossFit performance was ten percent better from offshore to onshore. The environment made a significant difference. I was set up for success. No surprise, but a useful reference as an example of suitable surroundings for success.

Environment is not just affected but physical layout and access to equipment! Leadership and team dynamics play a critical role as well.

Leaders should learn how to provide direction without steering the boat. Quality leaders know how to unlock potential without turning the keys themselves. The environment created by exceptional leaders is one which enables extraordinary results.

> *Leaders should learn how to provide*
> *direction without steering the boat.*

When people ask me what a high-performance team environment looks and feels like, I say it looks organised and it feels friendly. The delicate balance of professional and personable tends to encourage optimal performance.

A word that should go hand in hand with environment in a high-performance team, is 'engagement'. Leaders demonstrate vulnerability and inspire the psychological safety which draws engagement from the team.

I get asked how leaders can be vulnerable. Three ideas on that; share personal failures with the team, smile and greet members of the team, maintain open body language when talking to the team.

> *"Leaders with inclusive body language create an emotional environment that supports collaboration and high performance." – Carol Kinsey Goman*

According to Wikipedia, Fengshui is an ancient Chinese traditional practice which claims to use energy forces to harmonize individuals with their surrounding environment.

Fengshui tends to relate to the layout of a room, the placement of furniture, and the way a space energises our mood.

Energy is a critical element in any extraordinary team. Energy can be noticed and sensed, it is instantly recognisable in a sports team or a community.

The sun provides energy for our solar system. In the same way, leaders need to energise the environment so that each team member can blossom.

These are some simple examples and explanations about how to ensure an environment for excellence. Whether for yourself or your team, whether at home or at work, focus on the Fengshui to fare better in future.

Atmosphere

I'm in a good mood, how about you? If I ask you to think about what affects your mood, what comes to mind? Perhaps it's the weather? Or the family? Or work? Or progress? Or perhaps nothing comes to mind because you're not in the mood to think about it!

Research has shown that happier people live longer, and that mood has a strong effect on productivity. Do you ever wonder how you can set a more consistently positive mood? And when I ask that, do you think of your own mood, or the impact of your mood on others?

When it comes to striving for excellence, my experience and research has shown that whilst we understand the need for a performance method, and we have probably heard about the importance of growth-mindset, very few of us understand the significance of mood or moodset. Mood is the magic in this mix, and it helps us unleash mastery.

Standing on the shoulders of giants I proposed a simple model to help project managers better master the people component of project delivery. The model balances mindset, method, and moodset, while integrating leadership, teamwork, and discipline.

Mood or moodset is where I consistently find so-called "low hanging fruit" or the opportunity for small changes when assessing team climates ahead of transformation campaigns. This fruit could be welfare, recognition, respect, recreational facilities, travel issues, career growth, or just a voice in the conversation! Closer attention to these dials on the performance dashboard can be a gamechanger for teams, but often these climate indicators are ignored by all of us leaders.

Have you been in a family when someone was in a bad mood?

Creating a climate in the house that improves the mood of the majority, helps the atmosphere, and keeps us happier most of the time. Happiness leads to productivity, not the other way around! This has been shown in many studies on the subject, and it is why the 'pursuit of happiness' has been misapplied by many. Happiness must be in place first, then significant gains can be made.

My impact on the family mood as a parent and leader is one hundred percent. A grumpy mood in a confined space spreads faster than COVID-19!

During lockdown I watched the Netflix series *The Playbook*. It pulls back the curtain on how some of the greatest sports coaches of recent times have created exceptional performance climates to inspire excellence and evoke flow for their players and teams. I noted the twenty seven ideas and distilled them to a top five; start with the truth, always be the underdog, seize our opportunities, together as a trusting team, forward to the finish.

Two great books I have read include *The Culture Code* by Daniel Coyle and *Primed to Perform* (and the idea of TOMO – total motivation) by two former McKinsey consultants. The big takeaways were these: Purpose is vital, but a safe place to play and develop potential is the secret sauce: A moodset or climate which encourages expression and learning.

> *Purpose is vital, but a safe place to play and develop potential is the secret sauce.*

Play! Playlists can change the mood in an instant. Playbooks can help us codify what excellence feels like. Playful is the best motivator for TOMO – science backs this up. Play is the number one best way to unlock a good mood!

> *Play is the number one best way to unlock a good mood!*

In the last decade, I have conducted dozens of performance climate assessments in many different areas of the world, on and offshore. Climate is a combination of the environment and the atmosphere. It is the team mood. I learned through immersion to gauge the mood at any installation within about five minutes. There were three elements that told me about the prevailing mood, and they never let me down.

1. Are visitors greeted spontaneously by those who see us, or are we ignored?
2. Is the site leader expecting the visitors or is the visit a total surprise?
3. Is there an organised, clean work-site environment, with observable energy in the body language of team members?

Courtesy, communication, and collaboration are noticeable and predictable indicators of moodset.

In the year 2000 I was a commando captain helping to restore peace in the West African country of Sierra Leone. A rebel army was advancing on Freetown, murdering, and maiming hundreds of innocent civilians along the way.

My role was to fly onshore from the commando carrier, HMS Ocean, liaise with the spearhead battalion on the ground, and then lead our mortar troop of sixty marines as we adjusted several targets to ensure indirect fire protection when the rebels attacked.

During that six-week campaign in a war-torn country there were many threats and risks outside of our control. But what we could rely on was our training and our trust; trust in each other, trust in the system, and trust in the motivation of the marines on the ground. In other words, we focused on what we could control to lead a successful defence of the capital.

When I reflect on that situation, I realise how critical it was to sustain the right climate for the troops to deliver excellence in a dangerous place; to manage the mood, or moodset, for motivation and morale.

Trust is critical for moodset and despite our geographic

spread during that campaign, the troop was positive throughout. Maintenance of morale is a principle of war. Managing mood is a priority during crises.

Trust provides peace of mind which helps a good moodset. Oxytocin flows when we feel trust.

Do you remember what it was like at school when you had a teacher or a coach who inspired a positive learning climate? He or she created the conditions for growth and grit.

We had a rugby and running coach at my secondary school who dared us to believe that we could defeat our own doubts to rise and face even the toughest tests of our character. He nurtured a climate of confidence. A moodset for excellence.

In fact, the only time he discouraged our 'daring', and changed his mood, was when anyone showed an active interest in his daughters who were out of bounds as far as he was concerned!

Great parents, teachers and coaches know how to maintain a mood which inspires effort, it inspires energy, it lights a fire inside. The right mood can fuel the fire while the wrong mood can extinguish the flame.

> *The right mood can fuel the fire while the*
> *wrong mood can extinguish the flame.*

High-performance climates have inspiring servant-leadership at the heart of them. The leader maintains a balance between the 'stand' and the 'field' to win the hearts of the team.

In my final year at school, I was the anchor for our house cross-country relay team. I was also ranked as one of the best runners at the school. When I received the baton, I felt the overwhelming weight of responsibility to take the lead and finish strong, instead I mistimed my charge to the front of the field and ultimately failed in my mission, I crawled across the finish line, then collapsed unconscious. I had let the pressure turn to panic rather than staying calm and clear.

I woke up with a drip in each arm and the suggestion that I should not participate in the individual event the following week. My dream of winning the senior cross-country title looked set to remain just a dream.

Thanks to the Sanitorium support, I rehydrated sufficiently for a return to sports in a few days but was initially despondent about my chances in the individual event given my recent collapse.

I felt progressively stronger and more confident as it neared time for the individual run. My mood improved dramatically. On the day of the race, I stayed calm and felt grateful for the chance to compete.

I got the strategy spot on and found myself in front with one mile to go. It was then a case of hanging on to the lead, crossing the finish line, and enjoying the fulfilment of a dream.

When I look back at that small achievement from my school years, I realise it is a big reference point for how to overcome adversity, find the upside in a downturn, and simply help oneself believe that success can follow disappointment. Inspiration and flow were in balance and my mood was calm and composed. Job done.

We all have inspirational reference points from our lifetime. Referencing these can boost our mood, especially when facing a new challenge. Serotonin flows from social recognition to help us evoke flow.

Mood is the atmosphere, the background music, the feeling we have about our habitat. It is inspired by the leader which could be ourself! Belonging cues and observable behaviours are foundational to team excellence.

Mood can transform performance, we have felt and seen that many times. The leader's mood affects everyone's mood. A bad mood leads to lower energy. Lower energy leads to below-average results.

Playlists help mood if selected by the team. In fact, play has been found to be the top direct contributor to total motivation. Giving the team a space and a voice is key.

A rotten apple needs to be removed from the barrel so as not to spread. Rarely but occasionally that rotten apple will be the appointed leader, in which case the mood can be infected until the rot is removed.

Rarely but occasionally that rotten apple will be the appointed leader, in which case the mood can be infected until the rot is removed.

A bad habit is also like a bad apple.

A courteous, communicative, collaborative community starts a good mood. Truth, trust, and transparency sets and sustains that mood over time.

Our mood, and our effect on others, is owned by all of us, all the time. The way we show up, our language including our body language, who we spend time with, and where we spend our time; all these factors impact mood!

One of the benefits of being a performance guide is that a bad mood in the work environment is simply not an option due to the role. We don't have the luxury of being grumpy at work! As a result, we must manage our mood to be available for those who want a sounding board and a listening ear. Away from work there must be an opportunity to relax and reboot.

So, I'll ask again: Can you set a more consistently positive mood? And can you impact the mood of others? The answer is a resounding yes. In fact, it is simple, not always easy, but certainly worth it!

Now set your mood to maximum!

Morale

There are three key reasons why morale matters on any performance improvement campaign.

1. Safety is paramount and low morale is generally linked to variable concentration and interest levels, which means that the likelihood of a safety incident significantly increases as morale decreases.

2. Energy and productivity is linked to positive attitude, which itself relies on good morale. By contrast, apathy tends to go hand in hand with depleted morale so better morale aligns with better output.

3. Collaboration relies on good team spirit. Team spirit is affected by team morale. Collaboration is essential for effective planning, execution, review, and learning, so without good morale, each of these elements will suffer.

This is a deliberate simplification of a bigger subject but hopefully it conveys the obvious; ignorance of project team morale is a risk, and ignorance of poor morale is negligent because good morale is essential for safe, efficient, and collaborative operations.

We continuously promote a 'one team - one mission' ethos on performance improvement campaigns and our clients regularly feedback that this noticeable impact on team morale is a top-three contributor to project success.

Clearly morale does matter, and we've been privileged to support client leaders in bringing it about on challenging projects involving new teams, new regions, and new rigs. We see it as a critical success factor in any performance improvement campaign and to this end, we have evolved our approach to ensure good team morale is always top of mind.

Morale is a subset of moodset. The two are intrinsically

linked. Better morale equals better mood, equals better climate for the team to perform.

At some point or another we should all confront the question "what am I passionate about?" or "what makes my heart sing?", "what work was I born to do?". We reflect on our achievements, our strengths, and ultimately what we are passionate about; posed another way, we ask "what inspires me?", "what stirs my soul?!"

A high performing team is one where all the team members feel that they are drawing on their strengths most of the time each day. It is one where team members feel that they have a voice and that their opinion really counts. It is also one where team members feel fully enrolled and informed. Stakeholders in the right environment will feel energised to contribute because what they are doing has intrinsic and extrinsic benefit. The narrative is about value not cost. In addition, there is a bond of trust and commitment: True collaboration.

A world-class performance coach helps project leaders create the conditions for this reality: Ideally each specialist should be able to focus on their piece of the puzzle, whilst appreciating the bigger picture thanks to clear communication. Supervisors should be inspired to unleash team potential.

The continuous improvement process should become business as usual because it intuitively feels right. Process excellence should be streamlined and driven by a performance coach who clearly loves this aspect of the role. This frees up the enrolled and informed technical experts to focus on their tools and their 'turn' on the critical path. Inevitably this leads to better project results.

Joining a new and diverse team with a healthy appetite for growth and then climbing the arduous climb to peak performance, whilst supporting others on the journey and telling the story along the way: That stirs my soul.

"When you see the view from the top of the mountain, you forget the pain of the climb!"

3

CULTURE

"Culture is behaviour at scale". (Bain & Company, Inc. 1996 – 2022).

Daniel Coyle (Coyle 2018) spent years researching the secrets of highly successful groups. He was interested in how people show they care, how excellent groups unlock true synergy, and what is most important in achieving consistent success.

In Coyle's book, *The Culture Code*, a key finding was that interaction is more important than individual skills.

Interaction is more important than individual skills.

Daniel Coyle visited and researched eight of the most successful groups in the world over a four-year period, and this is what he found. The top three criteria for success were these:

1. Build psychological safety: engender trust and belonging.

2. Share vulnerability: be transparent and show fallibility.
3. Establish purpose: clearly communicate and enrol others in shared goals.

Coyle contested that culture is created based on what we see rather than what is said. Words are noise whereas behaviour is action which shows whether we are safe and connected.

Over the last ten years, I have immersed myself in the business of accelerated improvement, supporting leaders and teams in the upstream oil and gas industry, to unlock their potential and exceed their expectations.

In parallel I have read and listened to scores of performance related books, while also writing four of my own.

My experiences and observations show that any competent individual or team can transform by implementing the right system to the point where best practice is automatic (Wigham 2020).

This requires mindset, method, and something I call 'moodset'.

Mindset is led by leadership! It involves openness to possibility, openness to objective assessment, openness to coaching, and a belief in better. It includes optimism and resilience in equal measure. Mindset is critical for initiative, then essential for acceleration to automatic.

Method is system-discipline. It requires an uncompromising adherence to proven process even when it is the last thing anyone feels like doing. The process may not be perfect, but it certainly works. Method allows repeated practice to become automatic.

Moodset describes the prevailing performance-climate. It includes intangible but invaluable behaviours and deliverables which maintain the right atmosphere for team excellence.

1. Mindset.

Dr. Carol Dweck is recognised as one of the foremost experts on mindset. Her students wanted her to write a book about her accumulated expertise in the realm of mindset, so she obliged and compiled her masterpiece, *Mindset* in 2017.

She unpacks the mindsets, fixed and growth. Fixed-mindset people view abilities and qualities as relatively unchangeable, whereas growth-mindset people believe that we can all change, improve, and learn through application and effort. Dweck's thesis is that we <u>can</u> change our mindsets.

She provides several examples of fixed and growth mindset behaviours. She explains that we are all a mix of both but that through awareness and increased attention, we can catch ourselves when we are holding ourselves back, and we can generate a growth-mindset approach to focus on what we <u>can</u> control vs what we cannot.

Growth-mindset leaders and teams get a thrill from what is hard and from trying hard to learn something over time. Indeed, continuous improvement journeys take time and require effort, they involve failure, but that failure does not define the team. The effort and the learning define the team.

Dweck's research showed that the following traits were noticeable at growth-mindset organisations.

Trustworthiness, commitment, loyalty, agility, creativity, innovation, risk-taking support, integrity, a culture of development, care for wellbeing, collaboration.

A growth mindset is effectively a belief in better. It is never content because there is always more that can be done, but milestones and successes should also be celebrated because that fuels the fire to become more, for ourselves, and for others. As I have heard said many times: "Consistent hard work beats complacent talent over time."

> *"Consistent hard work beats*
> *complacent talent over time."*

2. Method.

In his book, *The Barcelona Way*, Professor Damian Hughes researches a proven approach to creating a high-performance team culture as seen at the football club FC Barcelona.

I found it additionally interesting to watch the Amazon Prime series *All or Nothing: Manchester City* at the same time as I was reading this book because one of the central figures in both stories is Pep Guardiola; previously captain and coach at Barcelona, now manager at Manchester City. Any culture is driven by leadership behaviour so being able to observe as well as read about Guardiola's leadership was highly informative.

Hughes references five culture models.

- Star model - Real Madrid (hire the best players).
- Autocracy - Chelsea (rotate the manager).

- Bureaucracy - Liverpool (profit over performance).
- Engineering - Borussia Dortmund (logic and detail).
- Commitment - FC Barcelona (more than a club).

The book then goes on to unpack a Commitment Culture. A model for success in any team. The acronym BARCA represents five steps to achieve this.

- Big Picture - Camp Nou | Cruyff | Catalan (Identity).
- Arc of Change: Cultural Signposts - Dream, Leap, Fight, Climb and Arrive (Transformation).
- Recurring Systems and Processes - Constant Repetition gets the Message Home (Ritual).
- Cultural Architects and Organisational Heroes - Respected Role Models (Legacy).
- Authentic Leadership - Stand for Something (Leadership).

The bracketed words are my interpretations based on personal experience, of the steps that Hughes puts forward.

3. Moodset.

Hughes emphasises the importance of the environment; the atmosphere and the energy surrounding a high-performing team. He notes that it is more than twice as important as the actual technical training focus in any workspace (Hughes 2018). I call this 'Moodset'. Good coaches create the right climate for the team to perform.

> *Good coaches create the right climate*
> *for the team to perform.*

Cultural fit between the leader and the team is very important according to Hughes. It is often overlooked or assessed in hindsight. Using the right questions to assess the cultural fit of a leader for a team can help to get insight. Asking about preferred work environment, leadership style and values can help provide useful clues as to a prospect's suitability for the leadership role.

Authentic leaders articulate their priorities, then they apply consistency and transparency to all aspects of their leadership. Leading by example and honouring trademark behaviours is critical. Hughes references Guardiola's approach of placing guardrails to protect the right culture - a way 'wide enough to empower but narrow enough to guide'.

Guardiola's guiding principles or trademark behaviours were these; show humility, work hard, team first. Intuitively we know this is required to achieve excellence, yet too many teams allow ego to detract from collaboration and progress.

> *Show humility, work hard, team first.*

A commitment culture is about the journey, not the destination. It can be achieved by groups who are committed to doing what it takes.

True culture transformation requires world-class servant leadership, an inspiring and highly recognisable identity, the right rituals, and of course exceptional role models or 'first followers' within the wider leadership group.

Team Development

The stages of group or team development will continue to be relevant and important while there are groups of people collaborating to complete tasks.

Bruce Tuckman is widely regarded as the source of seminal work when it comes to team development. He created a model which defined the stages of team growth (Tuckman, 1965).

These stages are forming, storming, norming, and performing. Adjourning was added later (Tuckman & Jensen 1977).

In a journal article by Tuckman & Jensen, a table provides more insight into the elements of each of the stages of team growth, and the authors delve deeper into small-group development, offering a model to understand development stages.

There are four stages with structures for each based on the authors' literature review. This theoretical model is one which has been studied and applied when building teams.

Forming a new team and then progressing to performing

as a team, is a team that is transforming from one set of behaviours to another. This theoretical model helps leaders and practitioners understand the stages in more detail.

Bain Consulting (1996 – 2022) describes culture as "behaviour at scale", therefore a team's behavioural progression through the stages of group development as described by Tuckman & Jensen, could be viewed as culture transformation.

Upstream Teams

The concept of multidisciplinary teams is not new, but Van Der Vegt & Bunderson (2005) shed some light on the perceived sweet spot when seeking the right balance between team identification, team learning, and team performance in the Oil & Gas industry.

The authors conclude that diverse capabilities within a team do not necessarily mean higher performance.

The findings have relevance for team leaders and reinforce the importance of assembling the right balance of diverse expertise within a group, while also investing in team identification.

Takeaways include the necessity to aim for a moderate level of diversity, a one-team culture, continuity within the team, and an active interest in team-learning behaviour as indicators of culture transformation.

The O&G industry has an opportunity to improve in terms of knowledge sharing and team learning (Selvam et al., 2019).

It is important to have the right performance climate to encourage learning and sharing. There is emphasis on the significance of relationships, the importance of trust and the need to build a genuine team. The right climate allows enough storming, but not too much! Constructive challenge forges stronger bonds within the team.

"Such a culture turns an organisation into a learning organisation that promotes knowledge sharing." (Selvam et al., 2019, p. 1823).

The intangible benefits associated with knowledge sharing are significant factors for team transformation. There is a strong link between knowledge sharing and collaboration.

"Knowledge sharing builds interpersonal trust among employees. Furthermore, employees' engagement in knowledge sharing activities builds a bridge between colleagues and creates a collaborative environment."

'Norms' and 'routines' contribute to the norming stage of team growth and transformation.

The authors conclude that learning and development has a positive impact on staff retention which in turn accelerates organisational transformation.

A qualitative study of HSE (Health, Safety, Environment) culture was conducted in the UAE in 2018.

The key elements of a strong HSE culture according to this article include leadership, vigilance, accountability with responsibility, and resilience.

Interviews were conducted with thirty people who represented a diverse sample of experienced frontline workers.

A clear finding in this study, is the reinforced importance of mindset. Individually and collectively, the right cultural mindset plays a major role in HSE performance.

The second finding of note is the role of the supervisors in the success or failure of HSE initiatives. Leadership through action and engagement, in congruence with clear verbal and non-verbal communication, is a critical point for climate and culture. Poor communication is a contributing factor to past incidents in the region.

The third significant finding in this study, is that training is essential for the continual improvement of the HSE culture. It also provides a way to embed the right mindset throughout the group concerned, and it enables supervisors to lead engagement and communication in a structured way. The right mindset and method are linked through training discipline.

Unocal Corporation is an oil company that achieved remarkable results in deepwater drilling (O'Donnell, 2002).

In a journal article, the author defines and details the eight key areas of focus that enabled Unocal to achieve 'drilling excellence' on their drilling operations in different parts of the world.

The first four points are all about the team. Team staffing involved selecting and recruiting the right people for the project. Team alignment, commitment and integration followed, and the author describes the criticality of this initial focus. This readiness period cannot be cut short.

The journal article makes it clear that only once the right people with the right mindset, are in place, can the team then focus on a proven method to achieve excellence.

The method involves planning, executing, and reviewing in a rigorous and inclusive way.

"It is through this multi-dimensional, cross-functional

design and review process that we arrive at an optimised well design." (O'Donnell 2002, pp. 69-70).

O'Donnell's conclusion is that people and process are more important than technology on any deepwater drilling project.

He notes in his final section on performance; "Upon completion of this review of Unocal's eight-point drilling-excellence plan, technology is conspicuous by its absence." (O'Donnell 2002, p. 72).

Farooq et al (2008) examined the culture at ONGC using the OCTAPACE framework which was developed by Udai Pareek. This framework examines an organisation's prevailing ethos to understand more about its potential to develop a strong performance culture.

"Any organisation, in order to survive and achieve successes, must have a sound set of beliefs. If an organization is to meet the challenge of a challenging world, it must be prepared to change everything about itself except those beliefs as it moves through corporate life." (Farooq et al., 2008, p. 42).

The OCTAPACE framework developed by Udai Pareek consists of the following.

- Openness.
- Confrontation.
- Trust.
- Authenticity.
- Pro-action.
- Autonomy.
- Collaboration.
- Experimenting.

In this study by Farooq et al (2008), ONGC Delhi is assessed using the OCTAPACE instrument. The finding was that the organisation had an average score on the culture scale; specifically, ONGC Delhi had a lack of openness and collaboration.

The implications of the findings are notable in this exploration of culture transformation in upstream O&G. Transparency and teamwork are necessary to break away from being average, and to transform to excellence.

"Ethos that fosters honesty and trust, replenishes member's energy, builds collective strength, and develops an emotionally intelligent culture. Thus, a positive workplace atmosphere deriving out of the unique culture is worth developing, as it becomes the foundation of true organisational success." (Farooq et al., 2008, p. 48).

In a study of the application of lean thinking to improve operational safety in the O&G Industry, Yeshitila et al (2021, p. 133) notes: "The core philosophy and two pillars of lean thinking are continuous improvement and respect for people."

The core philosophy and two pillars
of lean thinking are continuous
improvement and respect for people.

The study emphasises the importance of teamwork and team trust with regard to continuous engagement and improvement. The authors of this study argue that respect for employees could be improved in the O&G Industry.

In another lean study, Rachman & Ratnayake (2017) note the cultural significance of enrolment: "Without buy-in from employees, the organisation will be unable to embed a culture supporting the lean concept. In other words, leadership and commitment by management are required to convince employees in all layers of the organization to trust the potential improvements offered by the lean initiatives." (Rachman & Ratnayake 2017, p. 326).

In a study of the adoption of technology in the O&G Industry (Roberts et al., 2021) there is reference to the importance of culture for progress.

"The organisational culture in which they work will influence all aspects of their decision-making process, driving motivations, attitudes, and risk perceptions. Most of all, leaders can direct organisational values, resources, and the way that technology adoption is embraced." (Roberts et al., 2021, p. 15).

Green & Keogh (2000) studied collaboration in O&G and note the following factors as necessary for successful collaboration: Commitment and example from senior management, clear objectives understood and accepted by everyone, understanding where the 'win/win' comes from.

"An essential feature of a collaborative relationship is that it should represent a potential win for all the companies involved:

- Stretch objectives.
- Change of attitudes, and behaviours.
- No-blame culture.
- Integrated team—no duplication of roles.

- Frequent and open communication.
- Training in collaboration and in developing new ideas."

"The drive was to create a 'total team' where everyone was valued equally, dispelling the 'them and us' viewpoint." (Green & Keogh 2000, p. 254).

Green & Keogh also reference projects that benefited from the involvement of objective, external accountability partners such as consultants and coaches, to help achieve culture transformation.

"Many successful collaborative relationships appear to use an external facilitator to assist with the processes of building shared objectives and of developing trusting relationships. Facilitators can help team members to identify and modify beliefs and behaviours that are barriers to new ways of working. The continuing involvement of a good facilitator after the initial phase can be a powerful aid to improved performance." (Green & Keogh 2000, p. 255).

Culture transformation draws on knowledge sharing, collective mindset, transparency, and teamwork. It also requires a positive atmosphere, ethos, enrolment, engagement, and can benefit from objective, external facilitation expertise.

Royal Marines

Benchmarking the best is always good practice. When it comes to high-performance teams, we don't need to look far beyond the British Commandos. In fact, it was for this very reason that the England rugby team sought help from the Corps ahead of their World Cup winning campaign in 2003.

So, what are key elements of Royal Marines culture? What can teams take away from the elite to gain a competitive advantage at the front line?

1. It is a 'state of mind'.

    From the outset, the Royal Marines are looking for attitude rather than aptitude. It is the former that will get you through the tough times, together. We have a quote on the wall: "tough times don't last, tough people do."

2. Serving something bigger than everyone.

   The project identity, legacy, traditions need to unify all team members such that no one man ever becomes bigger than the team or the mission.

3. Core values.

   The Royal Marines values are excellence, integrity, self-discipline, humility. Simple explanations are attached to each so that all marines know how to apply these values to daily tasks. The values are tangible.

4. Commando spirit.

   Courage, determination, unselfishness, cheerfulness; spirit is the x-factor, the ethos, it is the non-physical part of a person which is the seat of emotions and character; the soul. Marines aspire to embody these characteristics.

5. Personal and professional development.

   Royal Marines do not sit still. They are always trying to better themselves, learn new skills, achieve the next level of capability and influence to be a better asset to the team. Each marine, and team, aims to be the best he can be.

In summary, the Royal Marines can teach us a huge amount about a world class culture: Fundamental to their high performance is positive mindset, willingly serving the cause, tangible values, commando characteristics, and a tireless pursuit of personal and professional growth. Mindset for attitude, moodset for atmosphere, method for achievement.

I was privileged to be part of this extraordinary organisation for eight years. It was an honour to serve and what I learned about a high-performance team culture has been invaluable since.

All Blacks

In the context of performance, we cannot ignore the most successful sports team of all time. The All Blacks have a win rate of over 80 percent since the game went professional and over 90 percent in the last ten years!

There are as many reasons why other countries should be better than New Zealand as there are superlatives to describe the class of their rugby. Yet they continue to dominate in a way which very few other teams of any type can emulate.

The book *Legacy* by James Kerr explores and unpacks fifteen themes which differentiate the All Blacks culture and provide lessons in leadership for anyone willing to learn. It is one of the best books I have ever read.

Here are three ways that the All Blacks sustain their excellence.

1. Haka.

   All rugby followers enjoy watching the Haka before a test match. The Maori battlefield war cry is fixating and for All Black opposition it must be hugely intimidating. But more than that I think what project teams can take from the traditional Haka is the significance of the investment made in a ritual which has nothing to do with the specific technical skills required to win the rugby match.

   There is no doubt that the Haka gives the All Blacks a competitive advantage even though it does not involve a rugby ball, a pass, a kick, or a tackle. The Haka clearly enables incredible intangible integrity; it builds up the team to be truly greater than the sum of its parts. It inspires collective self-belief, fearlessness, and camaraderie. It is about identity, unity, history, legacy. It sets their mood to invincible.

   It sets their mood to invincible.

2. Continuity.

   Succession planning in the All Blacks has become world class since the beginning of the professional era. There seems to be an instinctive mentorship programme whereby older players and former players fiercely protect the All-Black brand and ensure that younger players entering the fray are inducted into this vital mindset: Players are required to leave the jersey in a better place than when they received it.

For project teams, the aspiration is surely to inspire experienced campaigners to mentor and model the requisite approach to achieve best possible results such that younger team members understand and revere the expectation from the get-go. Equally, mentors set the mood for team members by crafting a climate and culture that is positive.

3. Stamina.

A signature of many All Blacks victories, is the scoring of points late in the game to secure the win. They have a renowned 'finish strong' mentality. There are games where the All Blacks have displayed remarkable composure and concentration to string upwards of twenty phases together before crossing the chalk for an injury-time try. The point is that they clearly train stamina as a genuine competitive edge. When other teams are tiring or quitting, the All Blacks are shifting into top gear.

If project teams can use relevant training and experience to promote team stamina, we too can go the extra mile as standard to win more and fulfil latent potential.

In summary, the All Blacks clearly epitomise high performance, so it is worth studying them and adopting transferable elements to improve project teams. They unleash true potential through a unique identity which is held in the highest regard and passed on from one generation to the next. They also have a specific focus on stamina to finish stronger than all the competition and to get the job done.

I'm a die-hard green and gold Springbok supporter but there is no doubt the benchmark is All Black.

CrossFit

CrossFit provides lessons to business and life.

My experience with CrossFit Aberdeen (CFA) is that there are some key elements of the general culture and approach which have valuable, and transferable value for continuous improvement campaigns in any setting.

1. The most significant element is the sense of community which is built upon a shared passion and commitment to get better through determination and perseverance. More than that, there is a real focus on listening and learning from each other based on different techniques and personal triumphs over adversity.

2. Most crossfit boxes have their rules somewhere visible; these include two very relevant points for aspirant champions, a) leave your ego at the door and b) always be on time. At the top level in this sport there is a genuine humility and discipline which inspires the average enthusiast to strive for improvement.

3. What gets measured gets managed. There is a genuine attention to data and detail in crossfit; numerous apps have emerged which enable easy mobile capture and analysis of each workout such that comparison can be made with peers and personal history. Data analysis drives planning and programming while workout reviews contribute more data - this in turn drives quantifiable continuous improvement.

4. Encouragement and recognition where needed and where it is due, becomes second nature because it

is the right thing to do. Fitter, faster athletes make a point of cheering on less experienced enthusiasts as a matter of course. This engenders a sense of confidence, trust, and mutual respect throughout the community. The moodset in the CFA Box is conducive to exceeding expectations time and again.

5. Everyone clears up after themselves no matter who they are. There is a real sense that every member of the community contributes to the quality of the experience and the workout environment. This attitude, and action is led by the coaches. It underscores the fact that no matter how fit the athlete, the Box is bigger than any individual.

There are clearly some very transferable lessons from crossfit to a continuous improvement culture anywhere; create a community, drop the ego and be punctual, measure performance, encourage and recognise others, and serve the community to make it better! CFA is well led and well loved. As a result it is well known and has a long waiting list of aspirant joiners.

Exceed

There are some crucial agreements which high-performing project teams have in place to exceed expectations no matter what the weather outside. These principles should apply anywhere.

1. Meet regularly to maintain clear communication and team unity - meetings need to be short, valuable, and well managed with a clear agenda, chairperson and prompt, actionable output.
2. Measure and display performance; progress against agreed strategic objectives, and actual versus planned performance matters to everyone in the team, find a way to make it visible even if it is not always positive.

3. Draw on team innovation and creativity to continuously improve; low morale tends to emanate from a sense of disconnect and disempowerment. A sense of contribution and value correlates with higher morale.

4. Recognise team members for a good job well done; look for reasons to praise team members and keep them always informed so that they can contribute and respond.

5. Communicate effectively; this is probably the toughest and most important principle to achieve. It involves listening with empathy as well as building trust, yet genuinely effective communication is a competitive advantage in any team!

These principles are woven into a positive climate and are especially important during bad weather. Focus on unleashing the potential of project teams through process discipline, positive mindset, and a happy mood.

During an Exceed breakaway in 2014, the Exceed leadership team agreed our values. The acronym LEAD stands for Lead with courage, Exceed expectations, Act with integrity, Deliver world-class transformational results. This simple word – LEAD – has helped us survive a global pandemic and make multi-million-dollar decisions.

During the offsite session, our values were debated for days to ensure we agreed they were the best representation of our core beliefs. LEAD is woven into our Exceed brand and is literally at the heart of our culture.

Family

Like many people, I have been involved in team building for a long time; initially at school, learning how to get the best out of our boarding house, track relay and rugby teams, then in the marines, learning how to unite warriors behind a mission, in the corporate world as a workshop facilitator, and finally in the energy sector, striving for the secret to team success as both a project manager and performance coach.

I have been searching for the key ingredients of a high-performing team and whilst I will not claim to have found the perfect recipe, I will say that by reflecting on one other (much more significant) learning experience, I feel a breakthrough coming on. I'm talking about family!

Being a child and sibling growing up I had some appreciation of 'teamwork' to get things done. As a co-parent of three young kids, I now have a crystal-clear insight into the difference between average and amazing 'family-work': In a genetic family environment, when all family members discuss, and truly collaborate to successfully implement a plan, the sense of satisfaction is immense. When this family teamwork is performed under pressure against a threatening challenge, the bond becomes primal.

Maybe this is why elite professionals who are part of world class teams, talk about their community as family. It is effectively the highest honour that can be given to a generic team. Brothers in arms, band of brothers, #blood #family.

If we accept then that special team communities aspire to become a family, we need to explore what makes a special family. In theory if we understand this, we may have the key to unlocking world-class teamwork. We'll focus here on five key contributing steps to becoming a super family.

1. Sacrifice.

     This speaks for itself and in one word provides a perfect anchor for family actualisation. Parents and children in any functioning family understand that there is more than just themselves to think about, this means compromise on the personal wish list and involves serving other family members to maintain overall progress.

2. Support.

     The stronger the mutual support in the family, the greater the chances of family security and future growth. Being there for each other and particularly parents being there for their kids, is the foundation of trust, loyalty, and integrity.

3. Stability.

A confident family unit is built on a stable platform, an island of calm even when the surrounding seas might be somewhat rough. This requires reliable, accountable family members and a familiar home base. It enables identity.

4. Systems.

Spontaneity is important but there must be a fundamental set of guidelines and principles from which the family operates, this provides structure. Routines and check lists are generally followed as standard.

5. Success.

This can be measured in many ways, but it is vital for morale and for momentum. Celebrating success is central to a happy family and members are motivated to achieve more based on how they see success benefiting the family unit.

World-class teamwork is indeed a lofty goal. It continues to be the focus for millions of people and billions of dollars. There are thousands of books on the subject. Potentially it is naïve to try and simplify the concept, but I am certain that top teams talk about being a family, and family undoubtedly benefits from the five S's listed above.

Reunions and relationships forged during tough team campaigns bear out the link. From team formation to 'family' status can be a very long journey but the steps above at least provide a start.

Leadership

The concept of followership has attracted growing interest in recent times, and it is certainly a favourite topic of mine. Perhaps it is because I went to a traditional boarding school, or perhaps it was my time in the military. Either way, I feel that good followership is as important as good leadership. In fact, I'll go a step further and say good followership is good leadership.

There are a few well known quotes which remind us that it is not helpful to have too many people trying to be in charge. "Too many chiefs and not enough Indians" is one such quote and we can all relate to scenarios where there is conflict in the crowded head office, and a shortage of competent, motivated, productive followers at the front line.

While we quite rightly place significant emphasis on appropriate leadership, we often forget that the very concept of leadership requires followership: "Leadership is a process of influence between a leader and those who are followers" – a quote I have come across before.

When I was a young officer in commando training, we would deploy on field exercises and assume leadership and followership roles based on a schedule of command appointments. In an extreme scenario, one minute you might lead one hundred people, the next minute you could be following orders in charge of only yourself and your kit. If leaders did not lead and followers did not follow, the machine broke down – it was and is a mutually beneficial, symbiotic relationship in its clearest form.

While the commercial world is not as regimented as the Royal Marines, many organisations could still benefit from a clearer leader/follower paradigm. An example of what I mean could be picking the right fora to challenge a business leader's decision. It is not a case of following blindly but appointed leaders who have reached their position fairly, deserve and require followers to unite behind the agreed mission to collectively succeed. If followers have issues with the leader, it is important that challenges are conveyed at the right time in the right place.

In a family setting we can all relate to the confusion and frustration that can manifest when it is unclear who is leading and when 'followers' are uncooperative. What tends to work well is when one parent accepts the situational importance of following the other's lead and setting an example to the children regarding good followership.

Followership is defined as the ability or willingness to follow a leader. We often discuss how a leader inspires followers; however, we should also acknowledge the courage and leadership it takes to selflessly follow to help the team be the best it can be.

In 2016 I drove seven hours from Aberdeen to Sheffield to join a close friend who I have known for thirty years. We had entered the master's category of a paired crossfit competition called Inferno Racing. Between Saturday and Sunday, we competed in 7 workouts, and at the end of it all, we were fortunate enough to be crowned champions of our age group.

I reflected on the achievement as I drove back up to Aberdeen on the Sunday night. It was just another weekend on the calendar, but it was a landmark in my life. It was not an amazing athletic achievement however it was a great reference point for me in terms of perseverance, determination, camaraderie, and the difference between participation and podium in any endeavour. I'm referring to the dots that join up to a podium performance.

With the benefit of hindsight, there were three differentiators on this occasion:

1. Bootneck brother.

    My friend and teammate for this event is not standard issue. He is a winner on every metric. We joined the Marines together in 1992, and we deployed to the same unit together the following year. We have worked and trained together in many places including the operational front line. We always have long conversations about all sorts of topics but for the actual competition workouts there was not much need for dialogue; the simple unspoken pact was to go as hard as possible, to work for each other, and to never ever quit. Having this history and congruency turned out to be a significant competitive advantage for an event like this.

2. Start strategy.

Ahead of every workout, Dom and I would agree our rep scheme and outline plan. We would then confirm this five minutes before GO! Being clear about our collective intent proved massively important when the limbs began to lock. We were ambitious but realistic with our approach and it helped us focus when the competition was close and muscle failure was imminent.

3. Outcome ownership.

Process ownership is critical; it is within our control as athletes and professionals. The right processes will drive the right outcomes. It is for this reason that we reflected on our performance and position as the competition progressed. This helped refine our resolve and rationale for certain strategies, particularly in the final.

The final itself was a true test, more of willpower and belief than anything else. I felt exhausted going into it and had some concerns about niggling injuries and certain movements, however, it came down to trust in our collective refusal to fail so close to the finish. We left it all out on the floor and as we crashed over the line at the end of the workout, I was overcome with relief and respect. There was a true sense of satisfaction in finally getting a win after years of training and varying competition results.

We achieved high performance as a pair on this occasion. Key podium reference points for me were as follows.

- Being in a team which feels like family, there is extra commitment to the cause.
- Joining a proven winner has a winning effect.
- A winning moodset leads to a winning performance.

As a performance guide, I focus on people and process, it is nice to have a recent personal reference point which reinforces the fundamentals of campaign success.

The moodset of first responders is a great reference point for teams seeking high performance. As such, *Chicago Fire* while entertaining, is also intriguingly inspiring. There are some excellent examples of leadership, teamwork, and execution under pressure.

I am always struck by the way the show weaves classic conundrums which are prevalent in most team settings. Leadership decisions need to be made between the 'easy way' and the 'right way'; the former tends to merely postpone the 'tough call'. Teamwork is negatively affected by individual agendas which are allowed to evolve unhealthily. Execution for fire fighters is set against a backdrop of high risk, time pressure, and insufficient information. As such, mission command, trust, and superior training is critical.

There are three outstanding leaders depicted in Firehouse 51 but there is also a self-correcting team which will not tolerate 'average'. The performance culture is that of a close-knit family and their depicted reputation is legendary across Chicago.

The series is not real, but the leadership, teamwork and performance lessons are incredibly relevant to the high risk, high reliability, extraction-based industries in which I work as a performance guide.

Firefighters in general are some of the bravest, most selfless heroes around. I am grateful to all of them for their service and sacrifice. I'm also grateful for their mindset which sets the bar for new teams looking to be inspired.

Creating a team identity is an exceptionally important early step towards campaign success. Campaign teams usually comprise multiple stakeholders from diverse backgrounds. Individuals and sub teams within the campaign team have their own identities and organisational brands. Unifying everyone involved in a campaign by forging one common identity is vital for collaboration, cohesion, and commitment.

We feel that forging a campaign team identity is so fundamental to accelerated team integration that we have embedded it as one of the initial key steps when guiding a high-performance journey.

Identity is best represented by a unique visual brand or logo. To this end, we work with campaign team members to co-create a truly representative campaign brand of which the whole team can be proud. This brand can then adorn knowledge documents, presentations, posters and even Tee shirts. It is a discrete logo which will only ever be associated with a specific campaign and as such its future appearance can trigger memories and shared reference points for the relevant people, place, and time.

We talk about 'one team, one mission' because uniting

behind a common cause is so powerful. As Babe Ruth said: "The way a team plays as a whole determines its success. You may have the greatest bunch of individual stars in the world, but if they don't play together, the club won't be worth a dime."

We see this in the world of sport; it is just as prevalent in the world of commerce and industry. Forging, and collectively uniting behind a common identity, makes any campaign-team aspiration a lot more possible.

A conversation with my business partner, Ian, recently reminded me of this extraordinary idiom.

'Crossing the Rubicon' means to pass a point of no return and refers to Julius Caesar's army crossing the Rubicon river (in the north of Italy) in 49 BC. This was considered an act of insurrection and treason.

In this day and age, when we talk about 'crossing the Rubicon', we mean to take a decisive, irrevocable step.

Crossing the Rubicon in a personal or professional sense is basically a game changer, a paradigm shift, or a step change.

Julius Caesar went on to lead the Roman Empire once he had taken that step.

There is another famous saying: "If you want to take the island, burn the boats!" This inspiring quote also owes its origins to Caesar. The Roman General ordered the burning of his own boats when he saw his officers wavering before taking the coast of Britain.

Fitting that the leader who challenged safe thinking to cross the Rubicon, should defy safe strategy to harden the resolve of his men.

In both cases the reward outweighed the risk. It takes

courage to break the rules, failure may result, but fortune tends to favour the brave.

Perhaps it is time to cross your Rubicon.

Teamwork

I have been fortunate enough to conduct many performance culture assessments on heavy industry installations. This reminded me that I have now been involved in dozens of similar assessments in several sectors in the last twenty years, and there is one simple realisation which is reinforced time and again through observation, perception, data analysis and direct interviewee feedback.

The reinforced realisation is that even with old equipment and average process, a group of people with exceptional servant leadership and world class teamwork, will challenge, and often outstrip similar operations which boast newer equipment and more advanced methodology.

Of course, if you take an exceptional team and give it the best processes and most advanced technology, in theory the sky is the limit. In reality it is often the 'underdog' label which inspires a benchmark team. Nonetheless, a well-led community of willing and proven volunteers with the right mindset and skillset is always preferable to a thousand pressed or egotistical men who lack motivation, drive, and cohesion.

A well-led community of willing and proven volunteers with the right mindset and skillset is always preferable to a thousand pressed or egotistical men.

There are indeed world class organisations with the leadership, the team, leading technology, and a trail breaking approach. Great examples from which we should all try to learn.

Sadly, all too often I have encountered the flip side, new installations with the latest hardware and software, but a dysfunctional group of people. Without exception in these cases there will be inconsistent and generally poor leadership, there will also be a collection of individuals, often capable, but who have not yet gelled as a cohesive unit, and who are not yet striving to achieve a clear mission, together.

My view is that it can be extremely difficult to help build a high-performing operation, there is no doubting that. But the first step as with any transformation journey, is admission. Admission that people are the most important component of any performance. Unless an investment is made in building a committed and well-led team, high performance will remain an elusive goal.

Unless an investment is made in building
a committed and well-led team, high
performance will remain an elusive goal.

What are some of the subtle behavioural indicators of a true team in any setting; a team likely to achieve a high-performance culture based on my observations and experience?

1. The first element is basic courtesy.

    This is such a fundamental one. It manifests in various daily interfaces such as greeting colleagues when you see them and responding to communications in a timely fashion. It needs to be a two-way street. If it feels like one party is constantly having to initiate the courtesy, there is no true team.

2. The second element is basic trust.

    This builds on courtesy. A true team has formed and 'stormed' to the extent that trust has been earned. It allows for personal growth and for individual expression to benefit the collective. If concerns about trust are regularly voiced, or micro-management is in evidence, there is no true team.

3. The third element is basic empathy.

    This builds on courtesy and trust. It means that team members are interested in the challenges of colleagues and that they seek to understand different points of view. If there is no sense that team mates genuinely care or can step into the shoes of others, there is no true team.

4. The fourth element is basic energy.

   This is an essential ingredient in any successful team. Energy can be seen and sensed, as can lethargy, an opposite element synonymous with poor performance and disjointed teams. If there is a lack of energy, there is no true team, at least not one that is likely to achieve high performance!

Bringing it all together, in my experience true teams consist of courteous individuals with high levels of trust, genuine empathy, and high energy. These elements can be detected in a relatively short space of time. Deficiencies in any of these areas will detract from team togetherness and prevent high performance. Get the basic elements in place and build a true team.

There is a well-known phenomenon whereby sports teams relax after just having scored, thus often allowing the opposition back into the game.

The same can be said for business teams who have enjoyed a period of growth, and then subconsciously slacken off through complacency and comfort.

Sustaining and maintaining performance at a high level is easier said than done. However, based on experience supporting dozens of high-profile frontline project teams, I'd reiterate that following these very simple (but far from easy) habits can restore focus when distraction comes along.

- Plan: whether it is a planning meeting before an operational phase, or a regular huddle before key decisions are made, planning is crucial for unity and trust as well as clarity and focus.

- Review: whether it is a sit-down discussion or a hot debrief post task, review allows for sharing and reflection which triggers awareness in the moment.
- Learn: whether a conference call or a crew shift-change, taking immediate action and rapidly applying lessons learned is a high-performance trait because it leads to quantifiable and positive change.

Top sports teams trigger renewed hunger in the heat of battle through an ongoing plan/review/learn cycle. Richie McCaw summed up this warrior mindset and general approach to maintaining focus on and off the field. In his movie *Chasing Great*, McCaw noted that every day, and after every score, he would 'start again'.

This trigger phrase would 're-set' the mind, the heart, and the hunger. Arguably the greatest rugby player ever, McCaw's approach may be worth modelling to combat complacency. The scoreboard is back to zero, the bank balance is back to zero, the hunger is back to huge!

The scoreboard is back to zero, the bank balance is back to zero, the hunger is back to huge!

Undoubtedly the most significant leading indicator of team success is the ability to transform in accordance to learning at the front line. This requires a well-led and hungry team, ready to give everything for the cause.

Change

Kaizen originates from Japan. It literally translates as 'change for the better'. In the 1980s, the driver of this approach, Masaaki Imai, introduced the concept to the western world.

Essentially it involves continuously improving through the deliberate identification and reduction or removal of waste. Toyota is often highlighted as a shining example of the benefits of a kaizen approach to manufacturing.

Kaizen emphasises the principles of incremental change and innovation. The authors of the book, *Kaizen* expand on a well-used quote to explain the concept.

> *"Rome wasn't built in a day, but the Romans continued laying bricks every hour."*

Quality circles and blitz exercises review and breakthrough on identified issues. The culture of openness to growth is key. There is always room to improve, and teams or individuals choosing to rest on their laurels, are likely to be left behind.

The *Kaizen* book draws a distinction between antiquated methods (companies like Netscape and Blockbuster) that should have evolved with new technology, and then proven values, which do stand the test of time. These include integrity and respect.

Proactivity, and guarding against procrastination helps to maintain perspective.

> *'Continuous improvement is better than delayed perfection.'*

Empowering all team members to speak up, and the 'crowdsourcing' of ideas, is fundamental to team improvement. Saving time and cost while removing waste or excess inventory from workflows is key. Simply questioning why something is done the way it always has been, is a healthy recommendation of the Kaizen culture.

> *'Target maximum return for the effort involved.'*

Kaizen recommends a focus on small steps, accepting that small failures are part of learning, improvement, and growth. Also recommended is a focus on fit for purpose. One hundred of the right words of any language would be enough to get by and could potentially be learned in ten days at ten words a day.

Note 'Parkinson's Law': work expands to fill the time available. It is therefore vital to allocate just enough time for the work required, otherwise inefficiency can easily creep in.

Note the 'Pomodoro technique': work in thirty-minute cycles (twenty five working and then five minutes of rest). This is considered optimal based on research into productivity and focus.

Note single tasking: computers cannot multi-task, humans cannot multi-task. There is a mental adjustment period involved when switching from one task to another. It therefore pays huge dividends to single task.

Note refresh and recharge: block time to go 'offline' and save mental energy reserves. Consider regular meditation (mental muscle building) and breathing exercises.

Note to lead through action and empathy: be patient, foster tolerance, correct people respectfully while finding process solutions. Maintain a well-motivated team.

'Recognise in public, rebuke in private!'

Note to follow the process: set goals, plan, execute, get feedback from accountability partners, and reflect on perceived areas for improvement. Journal, measure, learn, review, repeat.

The most important piece of advice for culture change is to take action! Interaction.

Conclusion

Moodset is about what we feel and sense, the atmosphere, the energy, the heart, and soul of a group in a certain place.

Optimising a team performance climate requires attention to detail, social detail. These details include cues and clues about team dynamics, team welfare, and team unity.

Culture is behaviour at scale.

Setting the right mood for our families and teams gives us a greater chance of being happy most of the time. This in turn enables the right collective behaviour which is a visible representation of our culture.

So moodset is critical for an excellent culture. It requires leadership and teamwork. Measuring and managing moodset will enhance mission-morale and motivation.

Reference points for hope and inspiration can be immensely valuable as we strive to sustain the best moodset for ourselves and our teams. Sensitivity to performance climate ensures we are tuned in to any concerns that require correction.

The success of our culture depends on the behaviour of our team members. Team members are looking for leaders to LEAD the way. Trust is a word that comes up a lot when reading about moodset, climate and culture. Build trust and we lay a foundation for progress.

Ultimately, we are all responsible for our own personal moodset. This then drives a strong collective moodset in the same way that we strive for a collective mindset. With this in place, our behaviour will likely LEAD to excellent results on a more sustainable basis.

So set your mood to inspired and change the world!

Author Biography

Tim Wigham grew up in Southern Africa and has dual British and South African citizenship; he served in the British Commandos for eight years between 1992 and 2000 before completing his full-time MBA in Cape Town, 2001.

Tim then specialised in the facilitation of SME executive leadership breakaways across a range of industries to build strong cohesion, as well as clear strategy, mission, vision, and authentic company values.

In the sports industry, Tim worked on mental toughness with several of the Springbok rugby players who went on to be World Cup winners in 2007.

Tim is currently the Head of Performance at Exceed in Aberdeen, Scotland. He has worked as a performance-improvement expert in the energy sector since 2008.

Tim was selected as a TEDx speaker at the inaugural TEDx event in Aberdeen in 2021. He is also a public speaker on performance climate, moodset, and inspiring leadership.

Tim commenced a professional PhD (DProf) by public works in 2021 with a focus on culture transformation in the upstream energy sector.

Tim travels, works, and lives between the UK and Southern Africa. He is married and has three young children. His main interests include Christianity, writing, reading, travel, and crossfit. He also enjoys blogging about inspiration.

About the Book

How do you set your own mood? If you are a team leader, a team captain, or a team coach, you also set the team mood. Do you understand how to continually improve in this critical role?

If you are a parent or guardian, the mood you set in the home and for your children is the legacy you leave for future generations.

Moodset is about what we feel and sense, the atmosphere, the energy, the heart and soul of a group in a certain place. Some call it performance climate. Moodset is as important as mindset for inspiring excellence.

Creating a climate for excellence is a never-ending pursuit so this book aims to stimulate ideas, and to share insights for inspiration!

The book draws on real examples, from school groups to elite military organisations, and from professional sports teams to offshore rig teams. The lessons learned from dozens of performance climates about how moodset drives excellence, will help you raise the bar and raise your game.

References

1. Copyright 1965 by the American Psychological Association. Tuckman, B. W. Development sequence in small groups. Reprinted with permission. This article appeared in the Psychological Bulletin, Volume 63, Number 6, Pages 384-99.

2. Coyle, D. The Culture Code: The Secrets of Highly Successful Groups. Random House Business, 2018.

3. Block, P., & Burnett Heyes, S. (2020). Sharing the load: Contagion and tolerance of mood in social networks. Emotion. Advance online publication. https://doi.org/10.1037/emo0000952

4. Oswald, A., Proto, E., Sgroi, D., Happiness and Productivity http://www2.warwick.ac.uk/fac/soc/economics/staff/academic/proto/workingpapers/happinessproductivity

5. Jones, T. (Director). (2021). *14 Peaks: Nothing is Impossible* [Film]. Noah Media Group.

6. Hughes, D. Humphrey, J. High Performance: Lessons from the Best on Becoming Your Best. Cornerstone, 2021.

7. Perry, J. The Ten Pillars of Success. Audible, Ltd, 2021.

8. Eastwood, O. Belonging: The Ancient Code of Togetherness. Quercus, 2021.

9. Tutu, D. No future without forgiveness. Rider, 2000.

10. Lomas, G. (Director). 2020. *Chasing the Sun* [Documentary]. SuperSport.

11. Asprey, D. Game Changers: What Leaders, Innovators, and Mavericks Do to Win at Life. Harper Thorsons. 2018.

12. Rothstein, L., Budd, M., You are What you Say; The proven program that uses the power of language to combat stress, anger, and depression. Harmony, 2001.

13. Avildsen, J. (Director). 1976. *Rocky* [Film]. United Artists.

14. Nelson Bolles, R., What Colour is Your Parachute: The bestselling job hunting book in the world. Ten Speed Press, 1970.

15. Collins, J., Good to Great; Why some companies make the leap, and others don't. Harper Collins, 2001.

16. www.gallup.com

17. Coelho, P. The Alchemist. Harper Torch, 1988.

18. Gracey, M. Director. 2017. *The Greatest Showman* [Film]. 20th Century Fox.

19. Eastwood, C. (Director). 2009. *Invictus* [Film]. Warner Brothers.

20. Berg, P. Producer. *Friday Night Lights* [TV Series]. NBC.

21. Singer, B. (Director). 2018. *Bohemian Rhapsody* [Film]. 20th Century Fox.

22. James, L. Producer. 2020. The Playbook [Documentary]. Netflix.

23. Doshi, N. McGregor, L. Primed to Perform: How to Build the Highest Performing Cultures Through the Science of Total Motivation. Harper Business, 2015.

24. Wigham, T. Accelerating Automatic: Lead Transformation, Inspire Performance, Coach Discipline, and Tap Into Team Flow. Author House, 2020.

25. Dweck, C. Mindset: Changing The Way You Think to Fulfil Your Potential. Robinson, 2017.

26. Hughes, D. The Barcelona Way: How to Build a High-Performance Culture. Macmillan, 2018.

27. Bain Consulting. https://www.bain.com/consulting-services/organization/culture-change/. Bain & Company, Inc. 1996 – 2022.

28. Tuckman, B. W. & Jensen, M. A. Stages of small-group development revisited. Group Org. Studies 2:419-27, 1977.

29. Van Der Vegt, G. S. & Bunderson, J. S. The Academy of Management Journal, Jun., 2005, Vol. 48, No. 3 (Jun., 2005), pp. 532-547 Learning and Performance in Multidisciplinary Teams: The Importance of Collective Team Identification Published by: Academy of Management Stable URL: https://www.jstor.org/stable/20159674

30. Brown, L., The Best of Les Brown Audio Collection; Inspiration from the world's leading motivational speaker.

31. Bennett, J. Bowen, J., Kaizen: The Kaizen Way of Continuous Improvement in Personal and Professional Life.

32. O'Donnell, Kevin. Unocal focuses on 'people' factors to improve deepwater drilling performance Oil & Gas Journal. May 6, 2002; 100, 18; ABI/INFORM Globalp. p. 65.

33. Al Mazrouei, M. A. Khalid, K. Davidson, R. & Abdallah, S. Impact ofOrganizational Culture and Perceived Process Safety in the UAE Oil and Gas Industry, Abu Dhabi University, Abu Dhabi, United

Arab Emirates. The Qualitative Report 2019 Volume 24, Number 12, Article 12, 3215-3238.

34. Ali, A.A, Selvam, D. D. D. P. Paris, L. Gunasekaran, A. Key factors influencing knowledge sharing practices and its relationship with organizational performance within the oil and gas industry. Journal of Knowledge Management Vol. 23 No. 9 2019.

35. Farooq, A. Sethi, S. Organisational Ethos and Culture at ONGC: An Empirical Study. Department of Business Administration, Aligarh, Muslim University. 2008.

36. Yeshitila, D. Kitaw, D. Jilcha, K. Applying Lean Thinking to Improve Operational Safety in Oil and Gas Industry. School of Mechanical and Industrial Engineering, Addis Ababa Institute of Technology, Addis Ababa University, Addis Ababa, Ethiopia. 2021.

37. Roberts, R. Flin, R. Millar, D. Corradi, L. Psychological factors influencing technology adoption: A case study from the oil and gas industry.

38. www.elsevier.com/locate/technovation. 2021.

39. Rachman, A. Ratnayake, C. Adoption and implementation potential of the lean concept in the petroleum industry: state-of-the-art Department of Mechanical and Structural Engineering and Materials Science, Universitetet i Stavanger, Stavanger, Norway. 2016.

40. Green, R. Keogh, W. Five years of collaboration in the UK upstream oil and gas industry. Strategic Change, June–July 2000.

41. Mastering "Moodset" to Improve Team Performance | Tim Wigham | TEDxAberdeen https://www.youtube.com/watch?v=PaEz5AXpgUk

Printed in the United States
by Baker & Taylor Publisher Services